T0355852

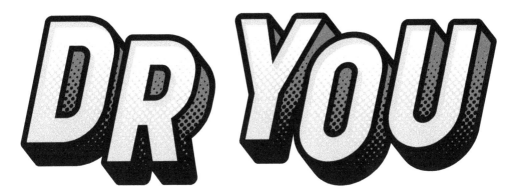

LORA MIRO

DR YOU

BECOME YOUR OWN ADVOCATE & TAKE CHARGE OF YOUR HEALTH

ForbesBooks

Published by ForbesBooks, Charleston, South Carolina.
Member of Advantage Media Group.

ForbesBooks is a registered trademark, and the ForbesBooks colophon is a trademark of Forbes Media, LLC.

Printed in the United States of America.

10 9 8 7 6 5 4 3 2 1

ISBN: 978-1-95086-352-5
LCCN: 2020907921

Cover design by David Taylor.
Illustrations by Wesley Strickland.
Interior design by Wesley Strickland.

This custom publication is intended to provide accurate information and the opinions of the author in regard to the subject matter covered. It is sold with the understanding that the publisher, Advantage|ForbesBooks, is not engaged in rendering legal, financial, or professional services of any kind. If legal advice or other expert assistance is required, the reader is advised to seek the services of a competent professional.

 Advantage Media Group is proud to be a part of the Tree Neutral® program. Tree Neutral offsets the number of trees consumed in the production and printing of this book by taking proactive steps such as planting trees in direct proportion to the number of trees used to print books. To learn more about Tree Neutral, please visit **www.treeneutral.com**.

Since 1917, Forbes has remained steadfast in its mission to serve as the defining voice of entrepreneurial capitalism. ForbesBooks, launched in 2016 through a partnership with Advantage Media Group, furthers that aim by helping business and thought leaders bring their stories, passion, and knowledge to the forefront in custom books. Opinions expressed by ForbesBooks authors are their own. To be considered for publication, please visit **www.forbesbooks.com**.

To the love of my life, my daughter Khali, who taught me the true meaning of strength and caring.

CONTENTS

INTRODUCTION:

DON'T CALL IT A WAITING ROOM; CALL IT AN ACTION ROOM

Hello, please take a seat;

the doctor will be with you shortly.

If you arrived here today feeling hurt or scared, then you've come to the right place—a place where true transformation is possible.

Nothing is certain but death and taxes … and getting sick. One thing all humans have in common is the inevitable experience of encountering a health crisis at some point, either our own or that of a loved one. In that way, health is the great equalizer—a universal, unavoidable challenge. By opening this book, you are taking the first step of one of the most important journeys of your life: the journey of learning how to become a true advocate for the well-being of yourself and all the people in your life.

Anyone who has suffered a health crisis knows that no amount of planning, exercising, or eating well prepares you for the moment your body seemingly betrays you. From my own experience with a series of ailments and injuries, I know that while you can't avoid this natural inevitability, you can be better prepared for it by understanding how your beliefs, choices, and environment play formidable roles in your well-being. When you understand these connections, you also understand that even though you may not always be able to prevent a health issue, you can always choose how to address it and how you can rebuild your life in the aftermath, possibly even stronger than before.

The path forward will differ for everyone and can be a long and arduous journey. But to begin all it takes is making one simple fundamental change. It's a familiar moment we've all seen on the silver screen and in books—the moment a small change in our environment or perception transforms a hero's world, much like the morning after the spider bites Peter Parker and he wakes up to discover his new superhuman abilities. It will take a lot of work and courage till he becomes the superhero known as Spider-Man, but that simple realization starts it all. Before any superhero can become, well, "super," they all need to do two simple things: (1) realize they are so much stronger than they ever thought, and (2) realize that they don't need to wait for someone else to come to the rescue—they can create change by taking action themselves. To take charge of your own health crisis, you need to make a shift and become your own best champion. From just a patient, you must become an engaged and active participant on your journey toward optimal health. You must become Dr. You.

Have you ever thought where the term "patient" comes from? The official answer is from the Latin verb *pati*, which means "suffering." But don't you find it an interesting coincidence that it is also connected to the word "patience"? In other words, a patient is someone who suffers patiently. This book is here to help you change that.

Though you may be here seeking certain goals—answers, resources, validation—you're here for your own unique reasons. Maybe you are here for personal interest, either your own or your family's.

Maybe you want to make better decisions and to educate yourself on how to live a healthier, more balanced life. Maybe you want to learn the right questions to ask your healthcare providers who support you so that you can manage your expectations for health and treatment. Maybe you are here to get real with yourself about your underlying beliefs and attitudes that affect your health.

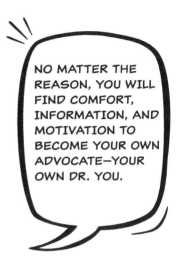

NO MATTER THE REASON, YOU WILL FIND COMFORT, INFORMATION, AND MOTIVATION TO BECOME YOUR OWN ADVOCATE—YOUR OWN DR. YOU.

You may be a patient disillusioned by the healthcare system, an individual with health issues, a caregiver, or a supportive team member trying to aid someone else with a health issue. You might arrive here because you are currently experiencing a health crisis. No matter the reason, you will find comfort, information, and motivation to become your own advocate—your own Dr. You. Those of you in supportive roles will learn how to advocate for another's care while also balancing your own needs. Whether you are experiencing a crisis or you are supporting someone who is, you will find the strength to be still amid the chaos and avoid making rash decisions.

You might be drawn to this book because you are seeking balance—maybe you spend too much time thinking of your health and all that could go awry. Maybe you always fear something is wrong with you or your loved ones. This book can help distinguish thoughts from reality—having physical symptoms, for example, does not always foretell disease. Many health experiences are simply natural aging processes or even emotional experiences. Conversely, you might discover you have unrealistic expectations of your body's abilities, resilience, or performance capabilities. These can be conscious or unconscious, but recognizing them and managing them without judgment can be truly transformative in your quest for optimal health. Through these chapters, you may find yourself seeking a way to challenge or confirm your own beliefs. No matter where you currently land on this spectrum, however, this book will be a useful guide toward finding your own balance, your own realistic baseline.

On the other hand, you may be a physician or healthcare professional who is looking for ways to motivate or engage your patients more in their own care. Perhaps you're here seeking to expand your understanding of how to position yourself to be a better resource to your patients. In this book, you will find a myriad of ways to improve service to your patients and their families—how to understand them better, approach them better, and ultimately use your years of science to support them better with personalized solutions every step of the way. Hard science aside, the journey held within these pages offers you the opportunity to gain perspective by focusing on the human experience of healthcare first and foremost. As a healthcare professional, I feel that if you're not asking yourself questions about how you can help individual patients feel better beyond a diagnosis, then you don't need just hard science; you need a mind-opener. This book will provide that.

No matter what brought you to this point, welcome. In addition to sharing my own healthcare and advocacy journey with you as a guide, this book offers answers, resources, validation, and some kick-ass action items to become the healthcare adviser you have always needed—Dr. You. Regardless of what brought you here, you will learn how to be your own advocate in the healthcare space and beyond. As you will learn in these pages, we are entering a time when self-advocacy is not an elective trait; rather, it is a necessary, mission-critical skill required for every individual.

It is time to leave the waiting room and enter the "action room." Prepare to meet Dr. You.

WHY DO WE NEED A HEALTHCARE SUPERHERO?

One of the most powerful indicators of a healthcare system's performance is its "amenable mortality"—that is, deaths before age seventy-five that are potentially preventable with timely and effective healthcare. Despite having one of the leading economies, when the World Health Organization (WHO) compared the amenable mortality of the United States with other countries, the United States ranked fifteenth out of the nineteen countries.[1] This research shows that the current model of care in the United States is falling short and is unable to care for individuals in the best ways possible. In fact, where other countries' amenable mortality declined an average of 16 percent over the study period from 1997–98 and 2002–03, the United States had a decline of only 4 percent. If the United States could reduce its amenable mortality to that of the top-performing countries, there would have been 101,000 fewer deaths per year by the end of the study period, sparing 202,000 lives in the two-year study period.

Research like this shows that the US healthcare system is falling behind other countries, and it's the American people who are losing their livelihoods and lives as a result. In making these criticisms, I stress that the answer is not about tearing down the institutions; rather, it's about active engagement both within and outside of the system. This book gives you practical, applicable ways to start being involved in the system tomorrow by becoming an active participant—Dr. You—in your own health and well-being today.

---

1   E. Nolte and C. M. Mckee, "Measuring the Health of Nations: Updating an Earlier Analysis," *Health Affairs*, Jan./Feb. 2008. 27(1):58–71.

After my own frustrating experience with the healthcare industry, I started seeing cracks in the system. I didn't need research to know that when I needed the system the most, it failed me. In the midst of my personal health struggles, I took a step back and considered my options: I could stay quiet and hope that my doctors would eventually point me in the right direction, or I could become an advocate who enacts change. In our culture's burgeoning trend toward agency and taking action, I knew that I needed to be open and brave about my options. I needed to objectively reflect on the path behind me and be deliberate in choosing the path before me.

I began asking my peers about their own experiences with the healthcare system, and as I suspected, their frustrations mirrored my own. They felt the same helplessness and powerlessness, and as an entrepreneur, I wondered how I might offer people the same agency I myself was seeking. This led me to consider diagnostic testing. What were its current limitations? And what were its potential opportunities?

During my research, I discovered a shocking trend in sexually transmitted diseases (STDs). Despite being preventable and treatable, STDs lead to lifelong consequences for many people and create a tremendous economic burden on our country. Though rates of "classical" STDs—gonorrhea and syphilis—are declining slowly in the United States, rates of many other STDs in this country far exceed those of every other developed country.[2] Since STDs most commonly affect people who are between the ages of fifteen and forty-four, this epidemic is of grave concern to my generation, who also happens to be the most economically productive group in our society.[3] Furthermore,

---

2   S. Aral, K. Holmes, "Sexually transmitted diseases in the AIDS era," *Scientific American* 264, no. 2 (February 1991): 62–9.

3   World Bank. World development report, 1993: Investing in health. New York: Oxford University Press, 1993.

STDs inordinately affect women more than men, and the World Bank estimates that STDs, excluding AIDS, are the second leading cause of healthy life lost among women between these same ages in the developing world.[3] Understanding these international comparisons dispels the myth that the United States is the leading country in healthcare treatment and services. Since this particular health issue affects my generation, especially young women, I decided to take action.

I knew from my own personal health journey that instead of trying to fix the problem by finding a patch, I wanted to start fresh and envision anew. So began my professional journey into the field of diagnostic testing. Along with a friend who was also an entrepreneur—and who would later become my cofounder—we discussed redesigning STD technologies from the ground up with the individual's needs, wants, fears, and expectations as a foundation. We didn't just explore other alternatives; we looked at all the options and decided it was time for a new alternative.

We live in a digital world where things happen fast: we expect packages overnight, we get messages instantaneously, we even see babies' faces months before they're born. Why don't we have the same expectations for our healthcare system? We wait months for a doctor's appointment, weeks for diagnostic follow-ups, more waiting for test results—all the while hoping our doctors will give us the magic answers we need to stay healthy. My partner and I decided to take the innovations of the e-commerce world and apply them to our antiquated processes and technologies for testing and treatment. We realized we could combine medical expertise with these digital processes and deliver them in the best way possible. This allowed us to redesign the way an individual interacts with these systems and give the power back to the individual. These discussions led to the creation of myLAB Box, the first company to offer at-home STD testing and the first ever nationwide testing-to-treatment platform.

Since the company's conception in 2013, I've been disrupting the status quo as a vocal advocate for a new approach to health and wellness well beyond sexual health: self-care. With this book, I want to portend what the future of health can look like if we take back our power, become our own advocates, and lead with Dr. You because, ultimately, self-advocacy is the only way to enact change.

TIME TO TAKE CHARGE

Whether we are prepared for it or not, we are taking part in a major paradigm shift. We are watching many of our institutions change, not only in healthcare but also in government, media, and environmental realms. As human beings, community members, and consumers, we can no longer afford to outsource our power and default to others.

A pendulum has been swinging throughout history between an individualistic, survival-of-the-fittest stance and an idealistic belief that the systems we've built with our intelligence and power are here to protect us and take care of us. As the pendulum swung toward the individual's role several generations back, we believed it was every man and woman for themselves, which is shortsighted and prevents us from leveraging our collective knowledge and combined resources to advance as a society. When the pendulum swung again more recently, we re-created many of our systems, assuming they would take care of us when we needed them. Our current history has shown this dependence is unwarranted and unwise. So what's the answer? Ultimately, neither scenario is ideal. One of them is completely disempowering and disenfranchising, and it always will be, because it requires you to surrender your own perspectives to the system and approach it with blind trust. The opposing scenario is also dysfunctional because by default, it negates the value of leaning on each other for support, expertise, and care. It puts an onerous burden on the individual, which is time consuming, costly, and unfeasible in the modern age.

Rather than swing back and forth, why not halt the pendulum and acknowledge that neither of these scenarios is serving us anymore? This book is about seizing the opportunity to stop the pendulum in the middle rather than swinging between extremes, so we can find a place of balance, harness our individual power, and redesign our interface with larger systems. Maybe some of those systems have been restructured in recent history, but ultimately, we have to redesign our relationship to them with agency and greater awareness of our own needs. Combining the best institution with the best intention and initiative is the only way to create lasting change and a sustainable future for us all, collectively and individually.

With the human population on the rise and waning amounts of resources, if we do not evolve and adapt, we will self-destruct. I don't intend for this book to be a doomsday prophecy, but I do believe this is mission critical. For this reason, when we speak of advocacy, we will focus on healthcare, but the same tenets apply to other areas: we need to reassess the way we are treating the environment and the way that we are treating ourselves; we have to consider the socioeconomic structures we created, which perhaps worked when we were a small tribe, but with more than seven billion lives at stake, it no longer does; we need to become engaged in all spheres because so many of our fundamental institutions are not meeting our needs. Being engaged in a way that is constructive and positive is particularly important at this point in history.

We're on the brink of a new era, whether we want it or not, whether we like it or not. Things have evolved and continue to grow at an unprecedented rate. If we're not active participants in these changes, then we will end up being stuck with systems that happen *to* us rather than *for* us. This is an opportunity to make sure that we have some voice, some say, some contribution to swing the pendulum in a direction that is not only good for us but is good for future generations as well.

This book will teach you to be your own health advocate, but on a much broader scale, it will guide you through a larger journey toward evolving into the society of the future. We will explore the individual's role in making these sweeping, fundamental changes. These personal shifts in thought are vitally important for the future for ourselves, our families, and our humanity.

Despite your reasons for being here, my hope is that this book will offer you a new perspective and clarity around what changes you can begin making today to better your life and health. Even if our views differ at the start, I know that by enacting even small changes, we can all get closer to a sustainable middle ground. In order for anything to have longevity, all perspectives need to support it, and sometimes the larger change we need to make as a society is a small one for the individual.

Using healthcare as a model for how to interface with a system larger than ourselves, we will push for empowerment, harmony, and balance, and for bridging divides. We will strive for empathy for self and for others, and we will seek awareness, enlightenment, and self-realization. We will begin a journey together with curiosity and wonder. This book will aid anybody who is searching for answers on how to live a happier, healthier, more empowered, and more successful life.

No matter what experiences brought you here, even if it's the scariest thing ever, be glad, because monsters can be our wisest teachers. Despite the negative stigma, it is my experience that questions, fears, and trepidations are the best things to happen to you because they force you to ask questions, seek the truth, and learn. If pain brought you to a point where you are seeking a new future for yourself and for everybody else on this planet, embrace it as the first step of the most valuable journey you will embark on. *Thank you for waiting. Dr. You is ready to see you now.*

CHAPTER 1:

THE JOURNEY BEGINS

BOOM-BAM-CRAAAAASH!

I felt I'd skipped time. My head felt like it hit a wall. There was dust floating in my car, and my ears were buzzing. Was there an earthquake? I felt a wave of nausea and pain sweep over me. What happened? I noticed my rear window was gone. I got out of my car and saw that my trunk was gone. Then I saw the car in front and realized I had been in an accident. My tiny GTI squished between a six-thousand-pound Land Rover and another SUV. People ran to me in slow motion. Head aching, back searing.

In 2010, I was a young, active resident of Los Angeles. Life was good and relatively carefree until that day, when, while I was sitting at a red light, another vehicle slammed into mine. Luckily, I was fine—at least that's what the doctor said. Still, in the weeks after my crash, I found myself struggling to perform daily tasks. I was unable to carry groceries, clean my house, or drive to work without severe pain. When I did try to drive to work, I ended up in tears from the agonizing pain in my back. Eventually, unable to make the sixty-mile daily drive to the office, I had no choice but to take a layoff and found myself unemployed. I went to another doctor. "You're fine," he also insisted. Still, my diminishing quality of life said something different. My car accident had completely altered every aspect of my life, including my financial livelihood. I was scared and panicked about what my future held. *You're fine. You're fine. You're fine.*

Anyone who has experienced a health calamity knows it is often accompanied by a myriad of strong emotions and challenging experiences. Even if you find excellent medical care and a diagnosis right away, there are still many stressors that can dramatically affect your life, like financial ramifications or continued access to quality care.

When I was faced with a medical crisis, I found the healthcare system confusing, expensive, and lacking in quality care. Many of the doctors I saw after my accident were dismissive, despite my undeniable and chronic pain. The trauma of a disease or an accident should be the worst thing that happens to you, not the arduous journey to recovery amid a broken national healthcare system. How did our healthcare system become so broken? Is it like this everywhere?

I grew up in Bulgaria when it was a socialist state. Under the ruling Communist Party, the healthcare system was equalized. You didn't necessarily always get perfect care, but the dynamics in play were much simpler and more straightforward. Furthermore, patients didn't fear financial ruin in using the system. Doctors weren't expected to turn a profit or look at their revenue. Patients weren't wondering what incentive the doctor had for making certain diagnoses or prescribing certain medicines. Doctors were focused on care. They spent as much time with a patient as it took. The patient's well-being was their measure of success.

I know that "socialized medicine" is a scary term for many Americans. It was originally used as a political weapon, and in that way, it's been surprisingly effective. The term gained popularity in

1947 when a public relations firm used it to criticize President Truman's proposal for a national healthcare system. As reporter and author T. R. Reid writes, "It was a label, at the dawn of the cold war, meant to suggest that anybody advocating universal access to health care must be a communist. And the phrase has retained its political power for six decades."[4] Considering that with each presidential election, the term "socialist" is spewed from many critics' lips as if it's an insult, the stigma clearly still exists today. Since we will be comparing many types of international healthcare systems throughout the book, let's remind ourselves that health issues need not be political debates. As we will discuss fully in chapter 2,

IT'S NOT A POLITICAL DEBATE; IT'S A GLOBAL CRISIS.

there is no way to heal our dysfunctional system without borrowing functional elements from systems in other countries. In fact, two of the most popular and successful examples of government-run systems already exist in our country—the US Department of Veterans Affairs and Medicare. Both have been successful and are quite popular with the millions of patients who use them. It's not a political debate; it's a global crisis. It's important to be objective and inclusive when finding ways to care for and manage our nation's people.

WHERE IT ALL BEGAN

When I was growing up in Bulgaria's capital city of Sofia, I lived a fairly idyllic life. Despite it being the largest city in the country, families rarely locked their doors. My friends and I played outside until nightfall when we were called in for dinner. If you were sick, you went to the clinic and waited. The medical process was quite easy

---

4   Reid, T. R. *The Healing of America.* New York: Penguin, 2009.

and foolproof. There was always a clinic or hospital nearby, and each specialist had his or her own office. It was much like shopping in a well-organized grocery store where each type of good had its place clearly labeled on the shelf so you could easily and quickly complete your shopping. In Bulgaria, you would visit the appropriate office, have services rendered, and then be on your way—no paperwork, no credit cards, no bills to haunt you after. It was truly that simple. I became quite ill with pneumonia at a young age, and I never doubted the care I would receive. There was never even a question of whether or not I would receive attention or whether my family could afford the medication. Though I had the physical discomfort of illness, my family and I didn't have the emotional stress of navigating a confusing system and paying exorbitant medical bills.

As kids, my peers and I were often involved in various community-wide health management efforts. This meant we would get vaccination shots together or, in the winter, we would play in a room while a UV light helped provide us with vitamin D that we lacked. There was an understanding as children under a socialized system that you were collectively being taken care of. Care was an integral part of our community. It was an unquestionable right. I took this assumption for granted, and like most things, I didn't understand its value until it was taken away.

What was most interesting about my upbringing in Bulgaria was that I was there as a ten-year-old in 1989 when the country changed from a communist one to a "democratic" one. The resulting chaos affected the country's systems from trash pickup to healthcare. Communism certainly wasn't paradise, but what I remember changing most were the centralized systems: animal control went away, police stopped doing their jobs, and crime became rampant.

Healthcare was perhaps the most drastic change. After the transition to democracy, you no longer knew where to go when you were sick. You'd go to the old hospital, where there used to be one office for each specialty, and now there were specialties missing, or there would be five offices for the same specialty. In trying to figure out which one to visit, you would discover varying prices for the same treatment, and oftentimes be forced to pay before care was rendered. Suddenly there was no consistency in the cost for services, the price of materials, or whether staples like bandages or disinfectant were provided. If you needed surgery, then you showed up at the hospital with your own supplies, sometimes down to the needle and thread, because you couldn't count on medical staff having them in the operating room. It was a corrupted system that meant you had to sometimes even bribe hospital staff to get the "nice" recovery room. Suddenly illness took on a new level of stress, unease, and perhaps most troubling, inequality.

When I was a teen, my cousin in Bulgaria was diagnosed with cancer. He was in his twenties. I remember hearing my aunt and other relatives problem-solving his care. "*This* doctor said we'd need to bring supplies to the hospital for the surgery." "Well *that* doctor said we'd have to pay extra each day for the bed, and we can't afford that." I saw them phoning their friends and relatives trying to determine if there was a better specialist somewhere. When my cousin's surgery was finally scheduled, I remember my aunt, mom, and grandma lugging bags of bandages and medication to the hospital to use during his surgery and postoperative care. Family and friends were very much involved in the whole process. How could we not be? Our safety net was gone, and we had to take care of ourselves.

Even as a young teen, I remember thinking, *Why did this change? What happened? Why is it so difficult to get medical care?* When I was a child and needed a dental filling, I'd go to the dentist and be out in thirty minutes; as a teenager, I had to worry about whether the dentist would try to upsell porcelain fillings. There was a new trend of practitioners trying to do procedures that weren't necessary, whereas this was unheard of before because there was no incentive. Back then it didn't benefit the dentist personally if you chose a different type of filling or opted to pull the tooth all together. Fast-forward a few years, and upselling had become an instrument for reaping riches previously unheard of in the medical sphere.

This sullying of the medical field deeply troubled me. Because I was a relatively healthy child and young adult, I felt little urgency to do anything about it at the time, but I remember understanding, even at that young age, that something integral to our quality of life was now badly broken. That *something* had to change.

As part of my growing disillusionment with my home country, I began devising my plan to leave Bulgaria when I was nineteen. I went to England first to become one of thousands of migrant seasonal student workers traveling to foreign locales to supplement their income. England was a different world. The West held promise for the order I had missed in my own country. For a brief minute, I thought I had left the instability of inefficient systems behind. Then came my first reality check.

I remember waking up early one Sunday morning in London with excruciating eye pain. Because I was a poor international student, I knew I was unable to afford urgent care. All affordable options were closed till Monday. I spent hours traveling across town looking for an open pharmacy or doctor's office. I was making phone calls and asking locals where I could find care—a doctor, a hospital, or a pharmacy. I felt so alone. By midday, I finally found an open pharmacy. I was drained and walked in, thinking I had finally found my salvation. I approached the counter and asked for eyedrops. The pharmacist asked, "Do you have a prescription? If not, you need to get one and come pick them up on Monday." I almost cried. I realized that no one was taking care of me—no government, no healthcare system, not even a doctor. The safety net of my childhood seemed like a dream at the moment. I finally understood how unique the healthcare system of my youth had been.

I understood that, even in an industrialized nation, I had to stay healthy because I couldn't afford to be sick. I decided then to make another change. Perhaps I needed to simply go farther West, across the ocean. Surely in America things would be different. I was determined to find a place that wasn't broken.

In my naivete, I still had a lot to learn about why things were broken and how they ended up that way. Ironically, in coming to the United States at the age of twenty-one, I ended up at the epicenter of the culture that created the problem. But this time I was an adult, and it was personal.

HEALING WHAT'S BROKEN

I didn't have many medical issues after arriving in the United States. This all changed after my car accident. After the wreck, I saw the inner workings of the healthcare system, and I was shocked by the level of dismissiveness I experienced from doctors. "Did you lose consciousness?" one doctor asked. I told him I had not. "Well it's obviously not a concussion then." *Huh?* I'm not a medical professional, but I knew it was possible to remain conscious and still be concussed. In trying to broach this concern with my doctor, he abruptly ended our appointment.

After this encounter, I was puzzled. I was still in pain, but the expert said nothing was wrong with me, so I kept driving to work and crying on my way home because of the excruciating pain. As I began missing work because of pain, I tried to convince myself there was nothing wrong with me, that it must just be some residual effect of the crash. After all, that's what the doctor told me. After more days of mounting pain, however, I realized I had to get checked again by someone else—someone more willing to listen and converse *with* me, not *at* me.

Despite the fact that my pain and symptoms remained, I continued to get more dismissive responses from doctors. I'd visit one doctor after another, and each time I'd walk out, thinking, *I'm not sure I completely trust this person's opinion.* As I went from doctor to doctor, my pain grew, as did my stack of doctor bills. The system was failing me when I needed it most. I was never used to getting second opinions before, but I found myself not only getting a second one, but a third one, and a fourth one, because I realized how important it was for me to find a doctor who was not only competent, but was also invested in the outcome of my care. That proved more difficult than I ever anticipated.

DR YOU

The process was not an entire waste, however, because with each visit to a new doctor, I became more informed. I realized that I would need to take control if I wanted a different outcome. I researched the doctors' backgrounds, who they were, what their training was, what their other patients were saying. I wanted to know what made *this* doctor different from *that* doctor. Was I going to the right specialist? Was I going to the right hospital? Quite frankly, it became overwhelming, and I wished there was an easier way. Even to this day, there really is no single centralized way to measure a physician's effectiveness through reviews or standardized quality practices. When it comes to the people we trust to handle the most important part of our life—health—this is a shocking lack of transparency. This makes the process that much harder for the individual seeking personalized care.

After a medical issue has been diagnosed, there is still a long journey ahead toward recovery. How do you heal? How do you fix what was broken? For me, that required an appropriate diagnosis, and I couldn't get a diagnosis until I could find a specialist I could trust, who seemed to care about my well-being, and who actually identified the root of the problem. If you think about any kind of human relationship, it's all about compatibility. Consider a person's optimal exercise instructor. Some people respond well to people yelling at them. They are motivated by a boot camp mentality: *Move your legs! Jump up! Twenty more! Don't quit! Push through the pain!* If you do this to me, I will probably get mad, punch you, start crying, or run away. Needless to say, it will not have a motivating effect. On the other hand, some people enjoy a more passive exercise routine: *You're doing great. Do what you can. If it hurts, back off. Deep, calming breaths.* I prefer to exercise in almost complete silence. Mention anything about chakras during my yoga class, and I'm out! We need to apply the same rules of compatibility we would use when searching for a physical trainer

22

or a potential date to selecting a doctor (in chapter 6, we will explore strategies for finding a compatible doctor).

As I became more willing to assume the active role I needed to take, I was eventually able to find the type of collaborator I needed. It only took four tries! On my first visit with my fourth doctor after my accident, I was pleased with the conversation and attention I received. I didn't feel like one of thirty patients, which was a profoundly validating experience for me. When patients have better, more efficient access to reviews and information on doctors, they can personalize their choice and thus accelerate their healing. During this visit, with a doctor I had hand selected *by* me *for* me, it was discovered that I actually had a hairline fracture of the spine. They also found compressed disks and other structural issues that were likely causing my pain. Though I was relieved to find the source of my pain, I was burdened by all I had learned about the healthcare system and how it contrasted with the model of compassionate and effective care I'd been raised to expect.

I chose to make a life and build a company in the richest nation on the planet. Why did I then have to spend dozens of hours trying to find a doctor who would listen and not rush me out of his or her office? Why did I feel unsupported and invalidated with each visit? There's no reason why I should have been driving to work for days in horrible pain if the first person I visited had taken the time to identify what was wrong, had that collaborative approach I sought, and had actually listened when I shared my experience. Rather than dismiss it, why couldn't physicians trust my perceptions and have a dialogue with me about possible solutions? This would have validated my experience and helped me develop confidence in the relationship I was building with my doctor.

WHAT IF?

Having grown up in a socialist state (I know; there's that "dirty" word again), I feel like I lived my early years in a parallel universe where healthcare didn't cost thousands and was operated by principles of empathy and wellness. After my car accident in America, however, my disillusionment with the US healthcare system felt eerily similar to what happened as Bulgaria moved to a democratic capitalist health-care system. I had that same unsettled feeling of being alone without a safety net. I thought the healthcare system in the US would be different, and it was, but was it any better?

While changing the system drastically in the immediate future seems unlikely, one thing we can change today is our strategy to deal with it. If we become more self-aware about our choices, and the role that we play as individuals in our care, it raises the expectations for physicians to perform at a different level. Doctors can then shift their role from godlike figures expecting blind trust to collaborators in care. The psychology that's been created in the United States has made doctors noncollaborative. Many doctors interact with their patients and their nurses in authoritarian ways that don't welcome or facilitate feedback. I think this dynamic can be quite damaging. Doctors need to be less like generals and more like coaches—wellness coaches.

When it comes to healthcare and human well-being, the primary driving forces should be care for others, community, and family. In a capitalist structure, there's no room for such feelings because if you can't quantify or monetize empathy, it becomes irrelevant. What if the world operated on these principles—doing right by others, taking care of each other, and ensuring quality of life? What if doctors only got paid when they kept you healthy and not when they treated you because you're sick? When a person experiences the trauma of illness or injury, how can we transform that into a positive experience? How can we take away the fear along with the pain?

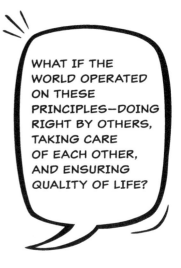

WHAT IF THE WORLD OPERATED ON THESE PRINCIPLES—DOING RIGHT BY OTHERS, TAKING CARE OF EACH OTHER, AND ENSURING QUALITY OF LIFE?

Having lived under several types of healthcare systems, I felt that the industry had captured and maintained my interest since early childhood. After my accident, the questions I posed became more and more in need of answering. What if we could use capitalism and beat it at its own game? What if we could create positive cycles around collaboration, empowerment, and empathy and monetize them, so they become things that businesses want to care about? If we could put a price tag on empathy and care, then we could create an incentive around those values. Then our discussions about healthcare wouldn't revolve around socialism, capitalism, or any other form of government.

The truth is we cannot change the system overnight, but we can change our expectations of our health professionals. We can become informed and engaged participants in our own health. I know how the standards of care can dramatically affect the psyche and the culture of a country. It's time to admit that our healthcare system is diseased, and in order to heal, we must diagnose the problem and enact solutions—stat.

EXAM NOTES:

➭ When faced with a health crisis, there are many other stressors that can dramatically affect your life, like financial ramifications or continued access to quality care.

➭ When a person experiences the trauma of illness or injury, we can transform that into a positive experience by changing the system and the ways in which we interact with it.

➭ Our discussions about healthcare need not revolve around socialism, capitalism, or any other form of government. There is no way to heal our dysfunctional system without borrowing functional elements from systems in other countries.

➭ When you want a different outcome, you must assume more control.

➭ We must diagnose our nation's healthcare problems so that we might heal and create a system that will take care of future generations.

2
//

CHAPTER 2:

WHAT'S THE PROBLEM?

Several years ago one of my college friends fell off a ladder and hit her head. Her parents, who did not live locally, called me to ask that I go check on her in the emergency room. After I arrived, I watched the doctors give her minimal attention until I mentioned that her father was a neurologist. After this revelation, the doctor perked up, and my friend ended up with an entire team surrounding her. I marveled at how this disclosure about her father's career would cause such a drastic shift in the quality of care she received. Furthermore, because I was the only one with her, they assumed I was family and gave me her financial documents at checkout. As we looked them over, I was dumbfounded by the costs. I knew she couldn't afford insurance because of a "preexisting condition," an eating disorder she struggled with in her youth. The thought of her being saddled with these exorbitant bills because of an accident that had nothing to do with a condition she had battled in the past seemed not only unfair but unethical.

Not long after, another friend of mine developed a mystery illness in his thirties. He quickly lost weight and began experiencing extreme physical challenges. He went to doctor after doctor and noted how little time each one spent with him before handing him a prescription and moving on to the next patient. Eventually, he ended up finding an unconventional concierge-style physician who worked on a cash-pay basis. At this point, my friend had spent thousands of dollars and months of compromised living before he was diagnosed with a complex combination of issues, including a fungal infection. Though the conventional doctors had diagnosed him with internal inflammation, they never dug deeper to uncover why this was happening. Luckily he was able to find a doctor who listened and worked to get to the root of the issue, but not before he spent a small fortune working with physicians who treated his symptoms but not their causes.

After my accident, I began to connect the dots between the similarities in my own experience and the health experiences of my friends and family. What I realized was that I'm not alone when it comes to grievances against the current healthcare model. In America, you hear an overwhelming number of complaints about doctors' busy schedules, insurance claim hassles, the cost of diagnostic testing, the amount of time it takes to receive a diagnosis, and more. With the vast majority of US healthcare—from pharma to clinics—structured to operate as businesses, wellness naturally takes a back seat to costs and profits. As a result, even the most caring physicians can get sidetracked by bureaucracy and eventually become immune and incensed about the people who are actually seeking their care. For example, a physician might see thirty patients in one day with back problems or back injuries. Whom do they pay attention to? Chances are they would prioritize a handful of patients they deem to be most needy or best fits for their practice. What about the rest? For the patient, this is the only back injury—their back injury. They are not one of thirty. It's their one life that is affected.

By capitalist theory, operating healthcare as a business should create better outcomes, but it has not necessarily done so. In the Organisation for Economic Co-operation and Development's (OECD) 2017 report, global spending on healthcare was $4,000 per person on average, while the United States spends almost $10,000 per person.[5] This spending trend does not seem to be slowing down either. In fact, the average annual cost of US healthcare increased more than 300 percent in less than twenty years, making it the most expensive in the world.[6] There is certainly nothing wrong with spending money on healthcare, as long as one is getting a return on the investment. Comparative research has shown, however, that this is not the case for Americans. The United States spends more than five times as much on healthcare per person as Estonia, but both have similar life expectancies.[7] Despite the increasing cost of the system, it has consistently ranked as the worst among industrialized nations in terms of "efficiency, equity and outcomes," according to a Commonwealth Fund report.[8]

It's not just the performance of the system that is lacking; it's also the financial strain it adds to Americans' finances. According to

---

5   OECD, *Health at a Glance 2017*, November 2017, https://www.oecd.org/ els/health-systems/Health-at-a-Glance-2017-Chartset.pdf.

6   Claxton, Gary, Matthew Rae, Michelle Long, Anthony Damico, and Heidi Whitmore. The Kaiser Family Foundation and Health Research & Educational Trust, *2018 Annual Survey*, http://files.kff.org/attachment/ Report-Employer-Health-Benefits-Annual-Survey-2018.

7   Emmanuel Akpakwu and Gabriel Seidman, "The $25 trillion healthcare problem and how to address it," *World Economic Forum* (May 24, 2018). https://www.weforum.org/ agenda/2018/05/25-trillion-healthcare-problem-how-to-address-it/.

8   The Commonwealth Fund, "Mirror, Mirror in the Wall," June 2014, https:// www.commonwealthfund.org/sites/default/files/documents/___ media_files_publications_fund_report_2014_jun_1755_davis_mirror_ mirror_2014.pdf.

a 2017 Gallup poll, the cost of healthcare is the top financial concern for American families, up 7 percent since 2013.[9] This is perhaps why I receive frequent emails from friends and family linking to fundraising sites that are almost always related to healthcare costs. According to Rob Solomon, the CEO of GoFundMe, the largest online, crowd-sourced fundraising platform, one in three of their campaigns is created to pay for healthcare costs.[10] This shows that Americans are less able to pay their health costs without assistance. In fact, the 2018 Common-wealth Fund Affordable Care Act Tracking Survey asked working-age Americans if they could pay an unexpected medical bill of $1,000 within thirty days, and almost 50 percent said no.[11] Let that sink in—half of Americans can't pay what is, by healthcare cost standards, a fairly inexpensive bill. What does that do to our families? How does that shift our experience? This is not a worry that falls solely on the uninsured. As Sara Collins, an economist studying healthcare at the Commonwealth Fund notes, insured patients report just as many problems paying medical bills as uninsured patients: "They also report not getting needed health care at rates that are nearly as high as those who are uninsured. So, it shouldn't be surprising that people are raising funds through crowdsourcing. But it really should be a deep concern for policymakers and providers."[12]

---

9   Andrew Dugan, "Cost of Healthcare Is Americans' Top Financial Concern," *Gallup*, (June 23, 2017). https://news.gallup.com/poll/212780/cost-health-care-americans-top-financial-concern.aspx.

10 "Daily Briefing," Advisory Board, updated July 30, 2018, https://www.advisory.com/daily-briefing/2018/07/10/gofundme.

11 Commonwealth Fund Affordable Care Act Tracking Surveys, Feb.–Mar. 2018.

12 Mark Zdechlik, "Go fund my doctor bills: Americans ask for help paying for health care," *MPRNews*, July 2, 2018, https://www.mprnews.org/story/2018/07/02/health-care-gofundme-crowdfunding-doctor-bills-minn.

As Collins points out, we wouldn't need to have these fundraising campaigns if the system worked. Furthermore, we wouldn't see so many Americans falling into debt because of medical costs. The number of bankruptcies due to medical costs is certainly on the rise, though the numbers are hard to pinpoint. A team of researchers led by MIT economist Amy Finkelstein studied the financial records of 780,000 people with health insurance and roughly 150,000 people without health insurance. They found that although the bankruptcy rate was about 4 percent for nonelderly adults, the financial ramifications were far reaching and devastating: "It doesn't mean there aren't really adverse economic consequences from adverse health. It just turns out they're not [strictly] about bankruptcy. They're much more about lost employment and earnings."[13] This was my experience after my accident. I didn't go bankrupt, but I did spend a lot of money on dead-end consultations and ended up losing my job as a result of the accident. The financial ramifications it caused affected me for years after the accident. Many of my friends also drained savings accounts trying to find diagnoses or treat accidents. This is money we could have otherwise invested into our businesses, families, education, or life experiences. Imagine what this diversion of funds can do to a generation—or a nation.

The ramifications grow even more disturbing when we look across the gender divide. Studies have shown that women, for example, are a lot more likely to be diagnosed with psychological or emotional issues when reporting symptoms, even in the case of a heart attack, negatively impacting the cost of their treatment or ability to even stay alive and further deepening inequality with a disproportionate economic burden. During their adult lifetime, average spending for women is nearly twice as high as for men.

---

13 Carlos Dobkin, Amy Finkelstein, Raymond Kluender, Matthew J. Notowidigdo. "Myth and Measurement—The Case of Medical Bankruptcies." New England Journal of Medicine, 2018; 378 (12): 1076 DOI: 10.1056/NEJMp1716604.

These economic consequences might also explain the recent trend of visiting other countries for healthcare services and pharmaceuticals to save money. A dental filling in Bulgaria, for example, costs about $10. When I recently went to a US dentist, they wanted to charge me $300 for a filling. Essentially, I could buy a plane ticket, fly home, have my dental work done, and stay on for several weeks and spend the same amount the American system would charge me. If a dental filling costs the provider $10, then why does another provider charge thirty times that amount?

When my cofounder and I were developing myLAB Box, we realized that we could provide STD testing costing between $189 and $269, depending on the number of panels tested. According to our research, the same level of testing done in-person at a doctor's office can cost between $600 and $1,800 without insurance. So where does the money go? What we've begun to realize is that the inflated costs that are being passed onto the individual are linked to the system's inefficiencies. In 2017 ProPublica published a series of articles on the leaks in the system and estimated that the US healthcare system wastes about $765 billion a year, which is about a quarter of what's spent.[14] With the consumer or insurers shouldering all costs, providers have little incentive to watch the bottom line. If costs rise, so do the prices. In response to these inefficiencies, the Institute of Medicine created a committee to investigate the dysfunction of the system and to provide strategic plans to strengthen it. The committee found the current approach of paying for individual services and products is what fosters this wasteful style of care. Instead, they recommend that "payments should reward desired care outcomes and movement toward providing the best care at

---

14 Marshall Allen, "A Prescription for Reducing Wasted Health Care Spending, *ProPublica*, December 21, 2017, https://www.propublica.org/article/a-prescription-for-reducing-wasted-health-care-spending.

lower cost. Payers should adopt outcome- and value-oriented payment models, contracting policies, and benefit design to reward and support high-quality, team-based care focused on patients' needs."[15]

CURRENT CRACKS IN THE HEALTHCARE SYSTEM:

⇨ *COST OF CARE AND ADMINISTRATIVE EXPENSES*

⇨ *QUALITY OF CARE*

⇨ *COVERAGE GAPS*

⇨ *INEFFICIENCIES*

⇨ *UNCHECKED REIGN OF PHARMA*

⇨ *IMPROPER SHARING OF COST BURDEN BETWEEN PROVIDERS, PAYERS, AND PATIENTS*

⇨ *CRACKS IN ENFORCEMENT*

⇨ *VALUES AND BIAS*

⇨ *IP-RELATED REGULATIONS OVER DEVICE AND PHARMA STIFLING INNOVATION*

⇨ *STATE AND FEDERAL REGULATION*

⇨ *LACK OF STANDARDIZATION AROUND THE BEST HEALTH OUTCOMES*

⇨ *HIGH RATE OF ERROR*

⇨ *INTERESTS OF STAKEHOLDERS THAT ARE NOT ALIGNED AND OFTEN AT ODDS BY DEFINITION*

---

15   Institute of Medicine of the National Academies, "Best Care at Lower Costs: The Path to Continuously Learning Health Care in America," September 2012, http://www.nationalacademies.org/hmd/~/media/Files/Report%20Files/2012/Best-Care/BestCareReportBrief.pdf.

As if the experiences of friends and family aren't enough, research now undisputedly confirms what many of us have known for years: there are major cracks in our healthcare system. This means the system isn't working for individuals and is therefore negatively impacting our economy and our lives. This is not just a financial issue; it's a life-and-death issue that must be remedied.

HOW DID WE GET HERE?

At the turn of the twentieth century, many people began looking outside their communities of healers and herbalists to seek the care of physicians. Vaccines were becoming more popular, and hospitals were becoming safer, which created a need for trained doctors. With the number of physicians growing in communities, people were more interested in higher levels of care. The only question was, How do they pay? Many doctors and patients devised various bartering agreements, sometimes involving livestock and other valuable goods. As historian Christy Ford Chapin writes, many doctors worked on sliding-scale payment systems that allowed lower fees for poorer patients and higher fees for wealthier patients. It was easy to see that paying lower sums more often was ideal for most families, rather than waiting for costly emergencies. Some doctors created systems that allowed for patients to pay a set premium for access, while some union welfare funds assisted other patients. Insurance companies did exist by 1913 when the tax structure changed, but they mostly offered group life insurance and pension plans for large businesses. Though some companies asked insurance companies to cover employees' health expenses, the insurers refused, citing the emerging field's riskiness and complexity. By 1938, the entire system began to shift as the nation fell into the Great Depression, and President Franklin Roosevelt sought to strengthen the relationship between citizens and their government. Fearing that the system would be "federalized," doctor groups finally agreed that some form of insurance was necessary. These early policies were "meager, stingy, [and] barely covered anything," according to Chapin. "The basic problem is the role that insurance companies have grown into," Chapin says. "It wasn't meant to be that way."[16] Though there were obvious problems with the system, they set the precedent that we're still dealing with today.

One of the founding tenets of America is its innate value of individualism. Here, the individual is bigger than the whole. Though this is touted as noble in most spaces, we must question whether it's helping or hindering the healthcare discussion. Having the individual reign supreme is fine in many areas of American culture, but in healthcare, if we think mostly of *I*, then there is no *we*. Healthcare is ultimately social and involves the well-being of a group and society as a whole.

16   Christy Ford Chapin, *Ensuring America's Health: the Public Creation of the Corporate Health Care System* (Cambridge: Cambridge University Press, 2015).

We must lead with the collective interests of Americans. This is why America often struggles in those times when policies need the whole. If we really are in agreement as a society that healthcare is a universal right and not a commodity just for the wealthy, we have a responsibility to ourselves and our children to make a change.

We must also be aware that we are in a new era when healthcare is of supreme importance because of the stress we are putting on the system through demographic and environmental changes. With almost seventy-five million people projected to become eligible for Medicaid by 2030, the system is about to be taxed like never before. Furthermore, our environment has altered, and it's affecting health trends, yet nothing in the healthcare model has changed to allow younger people—the ones experiencing the chronic diseases at earlier ages—to gain access to care. Are we not going to cover mammograms for women under age forty, even though rates of breast cancer have been on a steady rise? Are we not going to allow women over the age of twenty-six to receive HPV vaccines if medically relevant, even though we know it's the leading cause of cervical cancer?

In addition, changes in our environment, pollution, stress, and rapid industrialization are posing new dangers we cannot even begin to quantify in terms of long-term impact for our health. For example, despite the unknowns of wireless radiation's effects on humans, we are surrounding ourselves with 5G networks and cell towers at an alarming rate. Like the smoking hazards debate of the 1950s, it's going to take decades before current studies turn into meaningful action. But what if the early research is true? Then, like that generation of carefree smokers, we could have a generation of young people with brain tumors in dire need of a system that can provide the acute and chronic care they will require. How is the system preparing for our changing world? Spoiler alert: it's not.

LOOKING IN THE MIRROR

We are powerless if we are unprepared. Quite frankly, it's the younger generations who will be impacted the most. The Medicaid fund will be dried up by 2026, three years earlier than previously reported, according to a 2018 report.[17] What happens to our health in our later years? Who will take care of us? Now more than ever, it is imperative that we take on the healthcare system and lobby for changes that can respond to the evolving needs of Americans.

Inarguably, the healthcare system in the United States has many flaws. Perhaps the greatest defect, however, is the fact that it has remained relatively unchanged since its inception in the early twentieth century. If the system remains static, there is no evolution. As journalist T. R. Reid urges in *The Healing of America,* one way to change that would be to use the approach of President Eisenhower. When Eisenhower became president in 1953, the major domestic issue was the nation's transit infrastructure. The proposed plan that forty-eight states had already begun implementing was to have a network of two-lane highways that would run through the downtown Main Street of each city along the route. Rather than continue along the literal and metaphorical road more traveled, Eisenhower employed what academics later deemed *comparative policy analysis.* As Supreme Allied Commander during WWII, Eisenhower remembered his forward commanders marveling at the autobahn highway network in Germany. This was not a time when Americans wanted to borrow any ideas from Germany, yet Eisenhower understood the benefit of progress. As he wrote in his memoirs, "After seeing the autobahns of modern Germany, and knowing the assets those highways were to the

---

17   Paul Demko, "Medicare to go broke three years earlier than expected, trustees say," *ProPublica,* June 5, 2018.

Germans … I made a personal and absolute decision to see that the nation would benefit from it."[18] Eisenhower didn't set out to reinvent the wheel; he was simply open to learning from the success of others and not being too shy to acknowledge and borrow a good idea, even if it came from a foreign country.

We need to maintain this same open perspective and employ comparative policy analysis to borrow insights from other systems. This includes socialized medicine, a term that can send some Americans into fits of terror and conspiracy. As Reid points out, the problem with socialism is that it's foreign. He cautions us against the "American exceptionalism" mindset that doesn't allow us to admit that some countries do some things better than us.[19] He reminds us that it is not unpatriotic or anti-American to borrow ideas from other countries; in fact, the true patriot, he offers, is the person who recognizes the issues and tries to fix them.

Currently, the healthcare system is working against itself. To disrupt the current models of care, we must change our approach from short-term to long-term. I envision a future in which we can use predictive data models to optimize preventative screenings. Since 2014, laboratory service revenue is anticipated to increase 1.9 percent annually to reach $57.2 billion by 2019.[20] A lot of that testing is done on a reactive basis, meaning you're already sick, and in some cases, it might be too late. Considering that national health spending is

---

18   Dwight D. Eisenhower, *At Ease* (Fort Washington, PA: Eastern National, 2000), 167.

19   Reid, T. R. *The Healing of America.* New York: Penguin, 2009. 13.

20   IBISWorld, "Diagnostic & Medical Laboratories Industry in the US–Market Research Report," May 2019, https://www.ibisworld.com/industry-trends/market-research-reports/healthcare-social-assistance/ambulatory-health-care-services/diagnostic-medical-laboratories.html.

projected to increase by an average rate of 5.5 percent annually from 2018 to 2027 to reach nearly $6 trillion by 2027, imagine if we could shift even 10 percent of that money toward preventative screenings?[21] We would then see major decreases in downstream costs, not only for individuals, but also for the overall national economy.

Health insurance has been used in the system as a lever of power, a kind of golden handcuff for businesses and large corporations to gain advantage and attract (and retain) a workforce. Even to this day, it's hard for small business owners and individuals to take advantage of their bargaining power. We often overlook the fact that there are a lot more people collectively who are in small business, self-employed, or out of the system, than there are in the largest corporation, yet the benefits can be vastly different. The current model is set up to serve corporate interests. They've exerted every bit of power in retaining that because it has that much value in keeping the workforce dependent and attached to their employers.

Although my car wreck was a life-altering crisis for my health and finances, I often credit it for awakening me to the reality of a broken system and inspiring me to take action. As the Institute of Medicine concluded in its report: "Left unchanged, health care will continue to underperform; cause unnecessary harm; and strain national, state, and family budgets. The actions required to reverse this trend will be notable, substantial, sometimes disruptive—and absolutely necessary."[22]

---

21 Centers for Medicare & Medicaid Services, "National Health Expenditure Projections 2018-2027," February 26, 2019, https://www.cms.gov/Research-Statistics-Data-and-Systems/Statistics-Trends-and-Reports/NationalHealthExpendData/Downloads/ForecastSummary.pdf.

22 Institute of Medicine of the National Academies, "Best Care at Lower Costs: The Path to Continuously Learning Health Care in America," September 2012, http://www.nationalacademies.org/hmd/~/media/Files/Report%20Files/2012/Best-Care/BestCareReportBrief.pdf.

The first step toward a future with an evolved healthcare system that benefits the whole is to admit that the current system is broken. The second step is understanding that nobody cares more about your health than you do. That means that the power to protect your health is in your hands—only in your hands. There is no rom-com happy ending when it comes to healthcare. If somebody told you that during your next emergency, the fire department, the police department, and EMS will show up, but will leave you with an exorbitant bill that might haunt you and your family for years, what would you do? Would you shrug and go about your day? Or would you arm yourself with fire extinguishers, mace, first aid supplies? Would you still call 911 in need of help or try to solve the problem yourself first? And what holds the greater risk? You can't always rely on someone else to step in and fix all emergencies, and medical emergencies are certainly no exception. This can be a frightening and disheartening realization for many, but it also can be empowering. The person who cares most about your own well-being and that of your family is you. You can be your advocate. You can be your own hero.

EXAM NOTES

⇨ Understand how and why the US healthcare system is broken.

⇨ Healthcare is not just a financial issue; it's a life-and-death issue that must be remedied.

⇨ If a system remains static, there is no evolution.

⇨ Welcome a comparative policy analysis. Acknowledge ways that other systems are getting it right and serving their citizens. Don't fear these ideas.

⇨ You are powerless if you are unprepared. Get ready to be your own hero, your own advocate.

3
//

CHAPTER 3:

VITAL FOR SURVIVAL

I was never a "normal" kid.

Even from an early age, I was acutely aware of the resources required to take care of me. I was raised by a single mom, and I saw how hard she worked to support us. I remember Christmases when we didn't have money for celebratory foods. My mother was great at trying to hide this from me, but if you're a single child of a single mom, you're also her best friend, support system, and life partner. I saw it all, and I was extremely conscientious for my age. I just wanted to contribute. I didn't want to be a burden. I wanted to stand on my own two feet so my mother could worry about other things.

I remember being in grade school and deciding I would walk myself to school. My grandma was not in agreement, but one morning she finally conceded. I said "OK, great!" I grabbed my backpack and walked right out. On my trek to school, feeling emboldened and independent, I happened to turn around, I wanted to see the validation in the eyes of grown-ups around me about how cool I was walking on my own. Instead I saw my grandmother ducking behind a large trash can. It was like a comedy moment from a cartoon, but at the time, I missed the humor. "I see you behind the trash can," I yelled.

She called, "I'm sorry. I just wanted to make sure you got there safely. I promise I won't follow you tomorrow." Now I laugh and appreciate the kind gesture, but at the time, it infuriated me that she didn't trust my survival skills and maturity.

I got similar resistance when I announced at age fourteen that I had decided to get a job. My family tried to stop me. "You don't need to work. This is nonsense, you are too young," they said. And in many ways it was. None of my friends had jobs at that age, but I felt compelled to contribute to my family's resources. I wanted more than school offered—something that allowed me to take action and interact with adults. One day I decided to walk into one of the few corporate buildings in the neighborhood. I marched up to a man behind a desk and announced, "I want a job." Amused, he said he had newspapers that needed to be distributed. "Maybe you could find people who want to advertise in them," he said, chuckling. I took the papers and called out, "I'll be back later." I gave out all the newspapers that day. Soon I was selling ads in them as well.

From that point on, I was never without a job. It wasn't the money that excited me; it was the atmosphere, the dynamic interactions, and the opportunity to learn my own value outside of my small world of school and family. In my early teens, I worked for a medical supply company that sold natural dental products. I eventually took over their campaign marketing and scripted, recorded, and produced radio commercials and even drove their rebranding for the Spanish market. I managed business-to-business transactions and cultivated resale relationships. I didn't think much of this drive in my youth. I just knew I liked to be an active participant in the grown-up world.

I had always read about entrepreneurs and was invested in the alchemical processes they oversaw, but it didn't seem to have anything to do with me. I thought of them as superheroes who could solve problems and fix the lives of others. I remember my mother saying, "You can do anything you want when you grow up," but I never truly believed it. I didn't come from a place where I had the privilege to think that. I, like my peers, grew up with modest means. I didn't know many people who were rich or powerful.

It wasn't until the year following my car accident that I began to think critically about my early career aspirations. After the accident, I lost my job. This was the first time I wasn't employed in decades. What I realized was that it affected me on a personal level. It influenced my own feelings of value and worth. I spent that year focused on getting better. It was a year of treading water personally and professionally. Since I had gotten laid off, I was spending a lot of time thinking about my next career step. Because I was still in pain, commuting wasn't an option. Since I had always wanted to work for myself, I started opening up to different opportunities. Rather than put myself in a situation where I'd be potentially damaging my health further, I decided to accept my physical limitations and let prospects unfold around me. Surprisingly, as soon as I surrendered to this new mindset, I found multiple occasions to use my qualifications and experience.

For two years, I consulted with some dynamic companies. These were not massive, dehumanizing corporations like I was a part of before; they were creative companies with innovative ideas—video postproduction companies in the advertising and film space, architecture firms, start-ups, tech companies, entertainment, celebrities. I was finding value in what I was doing, and I was inspired by the innovative creators with fiery entrepreneurial spirits who surrounded me. I had found my people. In those two years, I witnessed firsthand how entrepreneurs come up with ideas and turn them into realities. Even better, I was an instrumental part in bringing these ideas to success leveraging my skills in PR and marketing to raise awareness and create demand where there was none before. After about two years, however, I started feeling dissatisfied by my new career path. I realized that I was still not personally creating anything new. I still was only furthering the visions and the ambitions of other people, and they were not necessarily what was most needed or important to me by any measure.

At the start of 2013, I decided it was my time. I believe in goal setting, and my goal for that year was to follow up on any idea that excited me. I would not be a passive dreamer; I would be a doer. Not long after my resolution, I met my friend Ursula for coffee. We were talking about life and dating. She had recently started dating again after her divorce and asked, "How do you deal with conversations around sexually transmitted diseases? What if you meet somebody you want to be intimate with? How do you even broach that subject?" We laughed about some of the awkward conversations and scenarios that could arise. Ursula mentioned that it would be helpful to have an app that would take care of these conversations for you. I answered, "That would be great, but the problem is most people don't know their STD status." Then something clicked. We started talking about why most people don't know their status. We realized that was the major problem. When the idea about personal testing came up, it seemed like an epiphany. *Why on earth is this not a thing already?* Why don't we use technology in this way? We date online, we buy groceries online, we book massages online, we buy flowers online; but when it comes to our health, we rely on systems that are outdated. Why would we shop at Blockbuster for our health when

> WHEN THE IDEA ABOUT PERSONAL TESTING CAME UP, IT SEEMED LIKE AN EPIPHANY. *WHY ON EARTH IS THIS NOT A THING ALREADY?*

Netflix exists? We left lunch with an idea that day, though we were certain there was *something* out there that was similar.

We spoke a few days later, and it was obvious we both had thought a lot about the conversation. Individually, we had each researched what was available on the market for at-home diagnostic testing, and neither of us found anything. Ursula was at a point in her career where she was exiting her second start-up and looking for her next idea. I had been living that year with my new mantra. If Ursula and I had had our conversation at any other time, I may have let it go, but because this was the year that I made that personal promise, we felt compelled to follow through. Luckily I was collaborating with someone who was as passionate as I am and just as committed to creating change and bringing ideas to reality.

With my experience in big e-commerce and the advances of online media, I knew this could be a revolutionary tool for healthcare access and personal empowerment. We saw an opportunity to combine what technology could do with self-advocacy, which could give a person unprecedented access to services that previously were only a part of the conventional brick-and-mortar model. Now that was something I could really get behind.

FINDING MY SUPERPOWER

My accident forced me to separate myself from my career. What I realized was that I needed to take time to cultivate my power outside of the value I brought to a company. This convergence of personal power, frustration with my healthcare experience, and my conversation with Ursula came together. It hadn't occurred to me that my healthcare experience wasn't singular. It was more of the realization of things that were horribly broken. *Why is this so bad?* It was when I talked with more friends and family and heard their similar experiences that I started thinking there had to be a better way, and maybe I could help find it.

I think what really motivated me in the conception stage of our start-up was the realization of how prevalent the healthcare problem was. I had found that the system didn't work for me, nor did it work for the people around me. Ursula and I had come up with a way to promote personal power that didn't involve the healthcare system. We had found a solution to a problem, and I knew it would work because I had experience in the e-commerce world. I had seen the trends and had paid attention to them. What I didn't know, however, was just how prevalent the problem was.

When we started researching more about STDs, we were shocked by what we discovered. Half of our population is estimated to be living with an STD, most without knowing about it. We inevitably came across research about the rates of infection, the insufficiency of diagnostic testing, and even the consequences of not getting diagnosed properly. This had far-reaching effects in people's physical and mental health, relationships, and even in child mortality. We hadn't realized STDs had such far-reaching consequences. The more we learned, the more we felt a sense of urgency to actually do something. We realized it had less to do with sex and more to do with the systemic healthcare management of generations.

Furthermore, part of our motivation in developing myLAB Box was to empower people. Unless you have to be dependent on something or someone, you should not be. Personal agency and freedom really is the first step to making life decisions that are positive. If you're always making decisions about your life out of your dependency on other things, you will never make the best decision for yourself. It's just not possible. I think much of my early independence was an attempt to free myself of any dependency on things. This was even my impetus for leaving Bulgaria as a teen. I thought, *No, there's another way.* You don't have to do what everybody does. You don't have to do what people tell you. I have an innate stubbornness that has always accompanied me. As soon as somebody told me, or merely implied, I couldn't do something, I became determined to make it happen—from walking to school alone to selling ads in newspapers as a child.

When I took this awareness of myself and applied it to the world around me—political systems, healthcare systems—I realized humanity's worst experiences occurred when individuals' power was taken away and they were forced to believe there was no alternative for them. If you believe that, then there will never be a revolution. I've always felt there's a way to be a hero, even if there is no war. Who's the enemy in the modern-day world? It doesn't have to be a foreign invader; it can be inefficient systems that take away your opportunity to live a good and healthy life.

BECOMING A SUPERHERO

There is a commonality between revolutionaries and entrepreneurs—both groups refuse to believe the lie that they must obey convention or be dependent on others. They don't accept the idea that there's no other or better option. They understand that personal power is vital for survival. They also are willing to try, even if the odds are against them. In this way, both revolutionaries and entrepreneurs are like superheroes. They are empowered and looking to serve and help others, and they are willing to disrupt the system if it means more people can get the help they need.

We should take a moment here to differentiate between two types of powers: personal power and institutional power. One gives power to the individual, and one takes power away. Thanks to comic books and the archetypal battle between good and evil, we see how unchecked power ultimately leads to evil because it lacks parameters. When nothing curbs its growth, it becomes greedier and all consuming. In world politics, if one country had unlimited dominance over all others, this would be considered tyranny. By having a balance of power, and by distributing the power, we can prevent tyranny from occurring—or at least give humanity a fighting chance.

Power doesn't have to be evil. It does not have to be about dominating others. In its purest form, personal power is about standing your ground and creating a balance that chokes out the self-serving authority of others. We must take our agency into our hands because if we don't, we're buying into the idea that somebody else needs to take control over our lives.

I am advocating that people find their power in terms of their healthcare, but the larger hope here is to just find your personal power, wherever it lies. Imagine a little bird in the nest that's used to its mom and dad feeding it worms every morning. Imagine if it never learns to fly because, since it's always well fed, it never has the impetus to learn how. The problem is, Mom and Dad are not going to be there to feed it forever. In a simple way, I think personal power is about self-sufficiency, about developing your moral compass, your belief system, so you can spread your wings. Without owning our personal power, none of these things are possible. We stagnate, we don't evolve, we don't learn anything. We can't fly. I don't think any species could survive without exerting a level of independence and self-agency. If we can become a society firmly aware of and grounded in our individual power, we can truly open ourselves up to innovation and creativity. Thankfully, there are things we can do to access, maintain, and cultivate our power.

HOW TO CULTIVATE PERSONAL POWER

⇨ **BE YOUR OWN PERSON.**

⇨ **BE INDEPENDENT.**

⇨ **DO WHAT'S GOOD FOR YOU.**

⇨ **LIVE WHOLEHEARTEDLY.**

⇨ **QUESTION THINGS.**

⇨ **EMBRACE CHANGE AND DISCOMFORT.**

⇨ **CONNECT WITH HUMANITY.**

BE YOUR OWN PERSON. My journey toward becoming my own person began the day I decided to walk myself to school. This mainly involved reaching outside of my comfort zone and claiming independence outside of the labels placed on me by others—child, inexperienced, fragile. What labels do you believe you have accepted that make you dependent on others?

BE INDEPENDENT. After I had that self-awareness, I cultivated more power by striving for independence. This relationship with dependence has changed a lot over the years. I think, initially, I didn't want to be reliant on my family as much. Eventually, I didn't want to be dependent on my school and their instruction on how to land a job. Next, I didn't want to be dependent on my company to take care of me or give meaning to my life. The older I get, the less I want to be dependent on institutions and broken systems. I've learned there are good ways to be dependent on things and bad ways to be dependent on things. Just like in personal relationships, there is a give and take. Lastly, I want to be less dependent on things that I perceive to be limiting, like the corporate environment in America, which is not geared toward facilitating the growth of young women or minorities. I couldn't think of a better way to do that than to avoid working where my value and my worth would yet again be determined by another. Sometimes, to change the game, you change the field. Making the decision to cultivate and maintain my own power is what led me to entrepreneurship. Now I can determine my own self-worth.

DO WHAT'S GOOD FOR YOU. The other ways to cultivate power are just as basic, though they require attention and dedication to the process. One is through discipline. It's pretty simple, really—just do the things that you know are good for you, like eating healthily, exercising, taking time to dream, spending time with people you love, making time to feed your soul.

LIVE WHOLEHEARTEDLY. Poet David Whyte once wrote, "You know that the antidote to exhaustion is not necessarily rest? … The antidote to exhaustion is wholeheartedness."[23] As soon as I read this, I found it to be completely true for myself. Even if I'm utterly exhausted from a long day, instead of going to bed, I try to do one thing that brings me joy. Some days that's something passive like watching TV or listening to a podcast; other days, it's painting or going for a run. Whatever I choose, I feel recharged afterward. The desire to pass out on the couch goes away, and I can find myself in a different space mentally and emotionally just by one simple gesture or action.

QUESTION THINGS. I also think it's important to always question things. This is not the same as withholding trust. We are in a dangerous cultural climate of questioning everything, even objective fact. There is a delicate balance here that must be achieved. You must question what is and always has been, but that is different than trusting nothing,

---

23   David Whyte, *Crossing the Unknown Sea: Work as a Pilgrimage to Identity* (New York: Riverhead Books, 2001), 132.

which has the dangerous potential to destroy things that have value. When we are diligent questioners, it allows us to see alternate ways of doing things. This creates space for creativity, innovation, and personal power.

EMBRACE CHANGE AND DISCOMFORT. Change is a fact of life. Spending any amount of energy to prevent change from occurring is like trying to prevent summer from following spring. What else could you use this energy for? The discomfort that comes with transformation is also not to be feared. If we were never uncomfortable, would we have a motivation to evolve? Change and discomfort are our allies and affirmations of our personal growth.

CONNECT WITH HUMANITY. Another obvious but profound way to access your personal power is to value those things that connect us, like empathy and love. There are daily ways you can tap into this powerful human source of power. Find ways to receive human kindness, and give it. Being cognizant of this interplay ensures that your personal power will be used for good. We all know with power comes responsibility. Heed the cautionary tales, and check in with yourself to make sure you are empowered for the good of yourself and your family, but not at the expense of others.

I think entrepreneurs and the self-employed specifically can really benefit from this lesson on power. As entrepreneurs, we could really change the values of our culture. If people who care about the well-being of others didn't start revolutions, but instead ran for office, started an ethical company, or bought a product from such a company, we could tip the balance of connectedness and power in our society.

Even if you're not interested in being an entrepreneur, you can still be a superhero. Don't forget that for all the things that divide us, we are all consumers. Consumerism can be seen as a real vice, but could we use that power for good? If you discover a product that is innovative and cool, research the company. If it is using ethical practices that align with your values, support it by purchasing the product. Reward those who are there to take care of you, who are actually making an earnest effort to make your life better. We vote with our money every single day. This is how change is created. The same should apply to the healthcare services we use.

I didn't come from a place in the world where you saw a problem and you did something to fix it. I came from a place where you were very much dependent on the institutions to take care of you. Growing up, I felt that power was something outside of you rather than something you innately possessed. It wasn't until I was self-reliant that I learned how to cultivate power rather than merely relying on it and hoping it worked in my favor.

I would have never thought growing up in a tiny Eastern European country, barely making it, that I would one day be the cofounder and CEO of a company that has created something that's the first of its kind in the American marketplace. In a way, I'm living that American dream. I didn't wait for a superhero to make it happen; instead, I became my own superhero and invested in the cultivation and maintenance of my own personal power. In real life, much like in comic books, nothing changes until we don our own capes and become our own heroes.

EXAM NOTES:

➡ When faced with a problem, use your own expertise and that of people around you to create solutions. If your solution could help others, consider sharing it through whatever means are available to you.

➡ Unless you have to be dependent on something or someone, you should not be.

➡ If you're always making decisions about your life out of your dependency on other things, you will never make the best decision for yourself.

➡ Find your personal power, wherever it lies.

➡ Sometimes, to change the game, you change the field.

4

CHAPTER 4:

MEET DR. YOU

I stared at the giant pills in my hand and thought of the tumultuous journey that led me to this moment: *Has it really come to this?* After months of feeling lethargic and weak, and hearing numerous doctors tell me I was fine (I had certainly heard that before!), I felt desperate to regain my optimal health. When had I lost it? How do I recover it?

A few years after my car accident, I found myself in another health quandary. I had developed insomnia, followed by an irregular heartbeat and pervasive fatigue. So far, conventional doctors had been of little help. After enough frustration, I reached out to an alternative medical practitioner, who declared that my issue was yeast-driven and could be eradicated by taking certain pills. Eureka! The catch, however, was that these miracle pills were not FDA approved; in fact, they weren't an actual medication. It was a combination of chemicals, the patent for which wasn't renewed by a pharmaceutical company and thus had become "public domain," so to speak. The practitioner assured me, however, that the pills held the power to get my life back. I stared at the giant pill in my hand a moment longer—here goes nothing—and then I took it.

Immediately after taking the pill, I got nervous. I thought, *What am I doing? This could be anything. What if I have a negative reaction? What if it causes more damage than good?* Like many people, I turned to the internet in a panic. I discovered that the pill I ingested was actually currently being used in veterinary medicine for the treatment of cats and dogs ... it was a powerful moment of realization. Was I really so desperate that I was taking animal medication?

By this point, I had been to numerous doctors seeking resolution, so why was I resorting to dog pills? Because in order to have my health issue resolved, I was still reliant on the expertise of somebody interfacing with the healthcare system on my behalf, and it was not working. Instead, I met numerous diagnostic dead ends and felt I had no advocate. I understood there had to be a better solution than experimenting on myself with veterinary cures.

As we've discussed in previous chapters, for a myriad of reasons, the current health model has created mistrust of doctors. We're unmoored with no one at the helm. This leads people to seek desperate measures in pursuit of better health. We go down rabbit holes of internet research into alternative therapies that might provide the one thing we are missing: hope. Hope for optimal health and well-being. Hope for the life we once lived or dream of living.

Self-care used to conjure images of gurus, supplements, and green shakes. These were fine treatments for nuisance problems that you could research and treat in "alternative ways," but when it came to deeper health issues that involved complex diagnoses or diseases, there seemed to be no real way to empower oneself without access to thousands of dollars. Hence me taking a dog pill! There are countless people struggling to find a better way after being let down by traditional medicine. Like me, most patients get frustrated with hearing "We don't know what's going on with you." Or worse, "You're fine." At this point, it's normal for people to start asking themselves new questions: *Why hasn't the doctor been able to fix this? What else is out there I could try?*

This is usually when people start to self-diagnose and self-treat with diet, lifestyle, and drastic body-hacking techniques. Thanks to the technological revolution, there's a lot of information out there to cull. For this reason, being your own health advocate has its advantages, but it also has its drawbacks because there are a lot of alternative facts, even when it comes to medicine. It's not easy to discern what are true and legitimate treatments and what are not. There are certain alternative measures that are OK to experiment with, like homeopathy and some diet changes. There are other things, however, that can really cause damage and long-term consequences. The key is to practice critical thinking so you can navigate the information better.

Even some doctors themselves have become more reliant on alternative methods of healing after seeing the limitations of conventional medicine. In an episode of the documentary series *Paleo Way,* clinical professor of medicine and clinical researcher Dr. Terry Wahls discusses her own journey beyond Western medicine. In 2000, she was diagnosed with multiple sclerosis (MS). Within three years of her diagnosis, she was using a wheelchair. After several more years of declining health using traditional medicine, she discovered functional medicine in 2007. She began researching the impact food has on health and created her own dietary protocol that excluded grains, legumes, and dairy while substituting in more vegetables and healthy fats. "That's when the magic began," she said. After nine months using food as medicine, she rode her bike for the first time in six years. "Clearly the paradigm that secondary progressive MS is only downhill is not correct, because I am getting better."[24]

As Wahls herself discovered, even having access to the greatest

---

24 *The Paleo Way*, episode 2:1, "Food is Medicine," directed by Rob Tate, featuring Pete Evans, aired on Netflix, https://www.netflix.com/title/81042978.

research and medical technologies available doesn't always lead one back to optimal health. Sometimes the only person who can navigate the path back to wellness is you. It's time to meet your biggest, most deeply invested advocate—Dr. You.

DR.

Join:
Expires:

ID NO:

I established my own relationship with Dr. You after my car accident. In the years following, as I experienced other health issues, I became more reliant on the role Dr. You played in my care. Several years ago, for example, I started experiencing growing bouts of anxiety, so I consulted my doctor. Not surprisingly, she prescribed me an anti-depressant. I knew from friends' struggles to wean off antidepressants that they can be a tricky solution to an already tricky problem. With Dr. You beside me, encouraging my participation, I boldly asked the doctor, "What about some simple stuff like CBD oil?" The doctor responded, "I really don't know how to measure the dose of CBD. Antidepressants are much easier for me to prescribe you because I know the exact dose you need."

Aha! His response showed me that sometimes a doctor's priorities are not the same as my own. His solution was the one that was perhaps easiest for him—not the one that was necessarily best suited for me or my goals. My concerns were for my well-being, my emotional state, and my long-term health. His concerns, on the other hand, were how he could quantify the dose and measure my progress. It wasn't that his concerns weren't valid or mutually exclusive, but in that particular instance, they just weren't necessarily aligned with my priorities or what I felt was in my best interest.

With Dr. You in my corner, I knew that I could dig deeper to find out more information about the drug my doctor was prescribing for anxiety. If I elected to use it, it would be because I had made a fully informed decision that it was right for me. I did some research and found that the prescribed medication not only caused a host of side effects while taking the pill, but it was also known for producing serious withdrawal symptoms after discontinuing it. Furthermore, I would have to take it every day for about three to four weeks in order to start feeling the positive effects.

Dr. You helped me see that I could perhaps start with something that doesn't have such hard side effects and issues like CBD. After all, the potential effects of taking "too much" CBD were minimal compared to the side effects for the prescribed pharmaceutical drug. Furthermore, if I was to wait a month for the prescription to begin working, were there any other actions I could take other than swallowing a pill—like maybe a daily hike or a brisk walk to boost endorphins—that could have a chance of creating that same difference or net positive? I was sure there were. I just needed to get fully informed to make the best judgments for my health.

If I had not done my due diligence and instead had followed doctor's orders completely, I would've potentially found myself much worse off in a few weeks' time. Luckily, I had Dr. You with me as my advocate and guide.

A BETTER WAY

The healthcare system has reached a critical moment of inefficiency that leaves many people thinking, *There's got to be a better way.* I have a friend, for example, who had to fight with her insurance company to keep her prematurely born baby in hospital observation. The insurance company didn't want to pay, so hospital personnel were essentially trying to force them out. In fact, the day the baby was to be discharged per the insurance company's orders, she suffered a cardiac arrest. Had she not still been in the hospital, the baby would have died. I have dozens of stories of friends and family spending precious time, energy, and money fighting with a broken healthcare system.

The honest truth is that you're not going to receive a fully informed decision every time you see a doctor. Medical professionals, no matter how good they are, are still subjective sources of information who operate from their own worldviews and from their own experiences.

FACTORS THAT MAY IMPACT A DOCTOR'S DECISIONS:

- ▷ **REVENUE**

- ▷ **KICKBACKS**

- ▷ **PERSONALITY**

- ▷ **REPUTATION**

- ▷ **QUALITY MEASURES**

- ▷ **PERSONAL PREFERENCE AND BIASES**

- ▷ **PERSONAL HISTORY AND QUALIFICATIONS**

- ▷ **CIRCUMSTANCES IN THEIR WORK OR PERSONAL LIFE**

- ▷ **PHYSICIAN'S PERSONAL WELLNESS EXPERIENCE**

There are other factors that govern your doctor's decision-making, and they're not necessarily all noble ones. Some of them are purely revenue driven. They have a practice, so they have to pay for the office, the electricity, the assistants, whatever else is entailed in that practice. That creates financial pressures that cause doctors to monetize their practices, often effectively turning people's health crises into quotas.

Perhaps one of the most fundamental flaws of the system that impacts all other inefficiencies is its structure—*we don't pay physicians when we're well, only when we're sick*. This model leads to a lot of economic dynamics that too often end

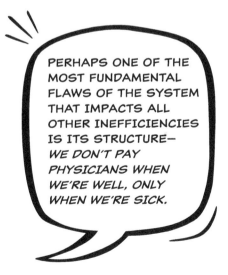

PERHAPS ONE OF THE MOST FUNDAMENTAL FLAWS OF THE SYSTEM THAT IMPACTS ALL OTHER INEFFICIENCIES IS ITS STRUCTURE— *WE DON'T PAY PHYSICIANS WHEN WE'RE WELL, ONLY WHEN WE'RE SICK.*

in doctors declining health insurance because it's costly and time consuming for them to actually get payers to pay, so they offload more and more costs to the patient.

Though there are many health practitioners who have their patients' best interests in mind, I would be remiss if I didn't mention that some doctors do get incentives. In fact, the 2018 payment reports released by the Centers for Medicare and Medicaid Services show $9.35 billion of disclosed payments made from pharmaceutical and medical device companies to doctors and teaching hospitals.[25] A Pro-Publica analysis of the payment reports found that "most" doctors receive payments, and those who do are, on average, "more likely to prescribe a higher percentage of brand-name drugs."[26] This unlikely partnership between drug companies and physicians has eroded trust across the entire industry. This dynamic has shifted the relationship between doctors and their patients: patients are seeking objective advice, but some doctors have already decided which medications they will prescribe based on the "agreements" they have with pharmaceutical companies. Of course, kickbacks are illegal, but, as ProPublica found in their analysis, some companies make "general payments" into fifteen categories that include promotional speaking, consulting, meals, travel, and royalties. When doctors receive these incentives from drug companies, it's hard to establish how much of their care strategy is actually for you, and how much of it is for them.

Furthermore, your quality of care is directly tied to a doctor's

---

25   Department of Health & Human Services Centers for Medicare & Medicaid Services, "Annual Report to Congress on the Open Payments Program," April 2019, https://www.cms.gov/OpenPayments/Downloads/report-to-congress.pdf.

26   Charles Ornstein and Ryann Grochowski Jones, "About the Dollars for Docs Data," *ProPublica*, July 1, 2015, https://www.propublica.org/article/about-the-dollars-for-docs-data.

personality and preferences. Strangely enough, these play a crucial factor in the care patients receive. How likely is the physician to look at alternative medicine—like acupuncture or talk therapy—as a care plan, for example? To treat only one part of the body, or one symptom, without addressing the root cause, is not the most effective strategy. These are sophisticated symptoms and systems, and they require a practitioner who is willing to seek guidance from outside his or her field. When I was younger, for example, I began experiencing chest pains. I went to numerous specialists without receiving answers. Finally, I went to one cardiologist who said, "I'm going to refer you to a rheumatologist." This seemed surprising to me and was confirmed when I went in for my initial appointment and the rheumatologist remarked: "I never get a cardiologist referring to me. Because of heart attack risks, I always refer to them." Because of the cardiologist's willingness to seek answers outside of his field, the rheumatologist helped determine that because of the way that my body was built and my high fitness level, I was straining and inflaming the cartilage between my ribs. When I was breathing hard during physical activity, it was creating spasms and pain. Because it's a physiological issue, I still experience it today, and each time, I think back to the doctor who wasn't afraid to send me elsewhere for answers. I let this be a model for the right kind of doctor to have.

A good physician understands that most symptoms are not isolated. They will speak to the totality of your health. I now have a doctor who follows this integrative philosophy. Sometimes I leave his office with vitamins, a chiropractic or acupuncturist recommendation, or some lifestyle and dietary changes. This type of physician has the highest chance of resolving my issues because he is not limiting himself by his own skill set and specialty. Imagine if you had a dam that is overflowing because too much water is pouring in. It's cracking from the pressure. Instead of figuring out how to manage the amount of water that's flowing into the dam, you decide to just plug the wall and continue building it taller to hold more water. This may work for some time but cannot continue indefinitely, eventually the structure will collapse. You might think, *Why would I do that? Why wouldn't I try to find out where the water is coming from, how to divert it elsewhere, or how to stop it?* It doesn't make much sense to keep building up, but unfortunately, this is how a lot of medicine works. Symptoms are often managed rather than their causes fully revealed and resolved. This is when your doctor's open-mindedness and personality can help or hinder your path to wellness. Is your doctor broadly informed enough to recognize when they're dealing with a complex scenario, and, if so, are they able to look to alternative forms of medicine? Or are they merely patching symptoms that will undoubtedly cause a flood of more serious ailments later on?

Just as we talked earlier about how unique optimal health is, the same applies to physicians. Let's say a physician has a certain body and is used to dealing with people with similar bodies. When an athlete walks in with a hurt knee and says, "I need to be at 100 percent," the doctor might measure that against her own 100 percent and respond, "OK, take some aspirin." Before my accident, for example, I was an active person. I ran and enjoyed long-distance bike rides. I'm not talking an hour on the saddle; I mean over one-hundred-miles-in-a-day kind of rides. I needed to get back to *that* activity level. Having a doctor successfully manage my pain wasn't enough. I needed the pain to subside, but I also needed to be as agile and active as I had been previously. I didn't need *any* life back; I needed *my* life back. During this frustrating time, I began to think about my own criteria for care. I realized I wanted to find somebody who worked with athletes or with people who were physically active, and who understood how important it is to fix things in a certain way, and regain as much quality of life as possible. I know that when we talk about my 100 percent, my doctor understands that I need to be at a certain performance level physically and mentally to run a business and stay active.

Many of us work under the assumption that physicians are godheads who should not be challenged. That's faulty logic and can be quite damaging to individuals. We should challenge the assumption that doctors know everything, because they don't. They have moods, illnesses, bad days, and personal struggles. So who knows what your physician has gone through or is going through, as they're consulting with you? Even the most well-intending physicians have hard days when they just want to get home to see their kids, not discuss a complex health situation. As humans, there will be times when your doctors are not in the best place to assist you. You might be given something and sent home just to get out of their hair. Obviously this doesn't happen all the time, but we do need to remember that doctors, like all professionals, are human and therefore fallible. Dr. You, on the other hand, works under a code of conduct akin to a physician's oath. The reality is that only Dr. You shares equal responsibility with you for your health outcomes.

DR. YOU'S ROLE IN HEALTHCARE

When it comes to your health, who has your best interests in mind? The only person who truly cares about what happens to you is *you*. No matter how informed a doctor is, there's nobody else who will be as passionate about your care and your well-being as you are. Dr. You is unlike any other doctor you're ever going to encounter because Dr. You knows your entire medical, personal, emotional, and psychological history, as well as all the nuances. Nobody else you will ever meet in your external life can do that. This is why you need Dr. You.

Dr. You should be an integral component of your healthcare journey every day, attending doctor appointments as your advocate, asking critical questions, and ensuring that a personalized health strategy is created that fits your life, your needs, your health. Dr. You validates that what you're being told and given is ultimately something that works with your lifestyle and worldview, and matches what you want out of your health plan. Dr. You is also there in between medical appointments, researching and becoming a well-informed partner on your healthcare journey.

In addition to being an advocate and a check for the doctors, Dr. You can actually enhance your well-being. In fact, being invested in your own health and healing process has been shown to positively affect outcomes. As patients certainly know and medical researchers have begun noting, the current model of doctor-led communications leaves patients feeling disconnected from their own healing process. Physician and researcher David S. Sobel has done countless research on the way communication and patient involvement affects health results. His findings show how ineffective and damaging this discon-nect can be for the patient, the industry, and the economy writ large:

> This critical mismatch between the psychosocial health needs of people and the usual medical response leads to frustration, ineffectiveness, and wasted health care resources. There is emerging evidence that empowering patients and addressing their psychosocial needs can be health and cost effective. By helping patients manage not just their disease but also common underlying needs for

psychosocial support, coping skills, and sense of control, health outcomes can be significantly improved in a cost-effective manner.[27]

Since Sobel's findings, researchers have tried to further quantify these improvements. In an observational study presented at the North America Primary Care Research Group conference, thirty-nine family physicians were chosen at random, along with 315 of their patients. Office visits were recorded and scored for levels of patient-centeredness. The study's findings were definitive: "The relationship of patients' perceptions of patient centeredness with their health and efficiency of care was both statistically and clinically significant. Specifically, recovery was improved by 6-points on a 100-point scale; diagnostic tests and referrals were half as frequent if the visit was perceived to be patient centered."[28] For the most part, humans are self-fulfilling prophecies. If you are disengaged, and if you are not involved in your healthcare process, you inevitably hurt your own chances for success.

In addition to the personal ramifications, patient disengagement burdens the entire system and can make conditions more expensive to treat. In *The American Journal of Medicine*, researchers found that lack of patient involvement "is associated with poor clinical outcomes, increased hospitalizations, lower quality of life, and higher overall

---

27 Sobel, David S. "Rethinking medicine: improving health outcomes with cost-effective psychosocial interventions." *Psychosomatic Medicine* 57, no. 3 (May 1995): 234–44. https://www.ncbi.nlm.nih.gov/pubmed/7652124.

28 Moira Stewart et al. "The Impact of Patient-Centered Care on Outcomes." *J Fam Pract.* 49, no. 9 (September 2000): 796–804. https://www.mdedge.com/familymedicine/article/60893/ impact-patient-centered-care-outcomes.

health costs."[29] This small shift in education and communication between the patient and the doctor has the potential to profit the entire healthcare system and the economy. Dr. You isn't just needed *by you, for you*—it's needed *by the entire country, for the entire country.*

The benefits of self-advocacy are undeniable and have been powerful motivators in both my personal and professional lives. Personally, I have taken more time to engage with and develop Dr. You in order to assume a more proactive stance for my well-being. Professionally, it led to the development of my company, myLAB Box. My business partner and I agreed that ultimately, people need to have access to their own care, and they need to take responsibility and control of it. This is the core of our business. Not only are we providing at-home health testing, but we are also freeing users from interfacing with a system that is not always meeting their needs.

When it comes to specific issues like STDs, it's clear that the system has failed. If it hadn't, we wouldn't be dealing with one of the biggest epidemics of our history. This is what made me and my cofounder want to start myLAB Box. We asked ourselves, *Why can't we do this better?* I can't tell you the number of barriers and obstacles that we had to overcome as we fought to create this company. We heard: "It's been tried before," "It's never worked," "Nobody's going to buy it," "You can't do this; you are not medical experts." Luckily, it's not in my nature to accept such limiting beliefs.

I recall reading about an experiment carried out in the late sixties by primatologist Gordon R. Stephenson. In his experiment, he took eight lab-reared rhesus monkeys and, one by one, put them in a cage with an innocuous kitchen utensil. If the monkey touched, chewed,

---

29   Deborah T. Gold and Betsy McClung, "Approaches to Patient Education: Emphasizing the Long-Term Value of Compliance and Persistence," *The American Journal of Medicine* 119, no. 4 (April 2006): 32–37, https://www.amjmed.com/article/S0002-9343(05)01201-5/fulltext.

or investigated the utensil, they were "punished" with a blast of air. It only took two to three times before the monkeys learned not to go near the utensil. Then, each monkey was paired with a "naive" monkey who had not been conditioned to fear the utensil. In these cases, the "demonstrator" monkey, through various ways like fear posturing, would warn the naive monkey not to touch the utensil. In one case, a demonstrator monkey grabbed a naive monkey by its flanks to stop it from reaching for the object. Stephenson concluded that "in six of eight critical tests sequences with pairs of socially normal lab-reared rhesus monkeys, behavior of one subject toward an object altered, with lasting consequences, the independent behavior of a second subject toward that same object."[30] In fact, when the naive monkeys were placed back in the cages alone, without the demonstrator monkey, they still did not interact with the kitchen utensil.

This is such an interesting and apt metaphor for how many of us approach institutions like healthcare. There is a sense of "Don't mess with it! This is how it's always been!" This is what's happened with some of the healthcare barriers we've discussed in earlier chapters. We've bought into the belief that change is not possible. My hope is to empower readers like you to take a more active and engaged role in their healthcare using the innate wisdom of Dr. You.

Dr. You needs to be a healthy questioner of the status quo. In other words, no matter how common a surgery is, for example, it has risks and might not be the appropriate strategy for you. Let's consider the common Lasik surgery. This surgery, approved by the Federal Drug Administration (FDA) in the 1990s, is also called laser vision correction and is performed routinely across the nation. In

---

30 Gordon R. Stephenson, "Cultural acquisition of a specific learned response among rhesus monkeys," in *Progress in Primatology*, eds. D. Starek, R. Schneider, and H. J. Kuhn (Stuttgart: Fischer, 1967), 279–288.

fact, roughly 9.5 million Americans have undergone the treatment. The fact that the procedure is a household name implies it's safe and effective. Dr. You's job, however, is to be your discerning guide who conducts extensive research before undertaking any procedure. In the case of Lasik surgery, Dr. You would discover in a recent FDA trial carried out with the National Eye Institute and the Navy Refractive Surgery Center that many of the patients are at a high risk for developing new vision problems after surgery: 28 percent developed dry eyes, and 45 percent reported disturbances. In fact, three months after surgery, 50 to 60 percent of all patients develop glares, halos, and double vision; after six months, some 41 percent still reported vision problems that interfered with their lives.[31] Are these odds good for comfort? Personally, I might wait till a better procedure becomes available on the market.

Always educate yourself through research, and don't be afraid to ask more questions. Any surgery that you do bears risk. Even if it is aesthetic surgery, like enhancing your breasts or adjusting the shape of your nose or your eyelids, any alteration or intervention carries risks that can be life altering. When I am faced with medical choices like this, I consider it a game of "Would you rather?" I ask myself, *Would I rather not have to wear glasses?* or *Would I rather have double vision?* These are difficult choices that should not be taken lightly. Understand that negative outcomes are possible. Think about how willing you are to take those risks because many posteffects can't be undone. By spending an hour conducting research, however, you can assuage your doubts and be assured that you are making the right decision for yourself.

Dr. You is not meant to be a replacement for doctors; instead, it

---

31 Roni Caryn Rabin, "Blurred Vision, Burning Eyes: This is a Lasik Success?" *The New York Times*, June 11, 2018, https://www.nytimes.com/2018/06/11/well/lasik-complications-vision.html.

is meant to enhance the care and effectiveness of the treatments you receive. Dr. You needs to always be there to ask the questions and advocate for your unique, personalized health. Dr. You asks practitioners questions like, "What can I expect from your proposed treatment? How soon before I see a change in my condition? What are the side effects of the medication you're proposing?" (See chapter 6 for a list of questions to ask your doctor.) As evidenced by numerous studies, being an active, informed participant in your healthcare not only reduces systemic costs and time spent with diagnosticians, but it also can have dramatic impacts on your quality of life and health outcomes.

THE FUTURE OF HEALTHCARE

In putting Dr. You at the helm of your care, you have the ability to shift the healthcare system to a model that better supports your needs. If you demand to be an active participant in your own care, this can have dramatic impacts on the status quo of healthcare. In essence, you are taking back your power. Even though it is a fairly radical shift, I think this is the next evolutionary step and will take us one step closer to being less dependent on a broken system that alienates us from our own health.

Because it's apparent to more and more people that there has to be a better way to do things in the healthcare sphere, what seemed like a radical leap of faith before is now just a leap of action. This seismic shift can happen through visibility and transparency. In many cultures, it's not polite or socially acceptable to talk about your health. It's not OK to talk about your digestive system not working well or your feelings of depression or mental instability. In order for us to shift an age-old paradigm, it will take all of us opening up and being transparent. We need to start paying a lot more attention to our human-to-human conversations so we can have more intimate moments of connection and vulnerability.

It's one thing to hear it from experts, but I think most of us change when we hear it from a friend or someone "like us." By sharing my story, I hope to make it easier for you to do the same. When we all speak up, our grassroots movement will transform the healthcare system. We need to find our voices and become more vocal about our experiences—speaking up about mental health, physical health, sexual health. We must take things out of the proverbial closet and talk about the things that we have marginalized and pushed aside. We don't need to fear change just because someone else tried and failed or warned us of consequences. Like the rhesus monkeys, we've been conditioned not to take on the big, scary industries that exert power over us. We can take hold of that which frightened the generations before us. We can take it in our hands, study it, and find ways to make it work for us.

What I'm proposing—and the company I have cofounded—may be unwelcome by many in the healthcare industry, and that's OK. I'm not here to coddle or appease. I'm here to shine a light on the truth, empower and embolden individuals to take ownership of their bodies, and to challenge—or at least question—the status quo. By using Dr. You, we are developing a more intuitive, self-directed approach to our healthcare, so we can replace the age-old system that is failing our families, our friends, and ourselves each day. We have the power to change the landscape of the healthcare model; we just have to be empowered enough to do it.

EXAM NOTES:

☞ The healthcare system has reached a critical moment of inefficiency that leaves many people wondering if there's a better way.

☞ Dr. You is not there as a critic to Western medicine, encouraging you to reject care altogether. Instead, Dr. You is there to make sure that the care you're getting fits your needs and lifestyle.

☞ The honest truth is that you're not going to receive a fully informed decision every time you see a doctor. Medical professionals, no matter how good they are, are still subjective sources of information who operate from their own worldviews and from their own limited knowledge base and experiences.

☞ Dr. You should be an integral component of your healthcare journey every day, attending doctor appointments as your advocate, asking critical questions, and ensuring that a personalized health strategy is created that fits your life, your needs, and your health.

☞ Dr. You is not meant to be a replacement for doctors; Dr. You is instead meant to enhance the care and effectiveness of the treatments you receive and become your physician's best ally in making sure you get the best possible care for your individual need.

CHAPTER 5:

THE HERO'S (HEALTHCARE) JOURNEY

Any time a person experiences a health crisis, it is the start of a journey, and it's rarely an easy one. Its universality makes it an archetypal experience that we all face on some level, at some time. Life and death, and the entire spectrum in between, are experiences at the core of humanity. We cannot escape our own mortality, though we can make some adjustments—both positive and negative—in its trajectory. In this chapter, we will look closer at the teachings that come with the journey, so that we might see the innate gifts that lie within.

Comparative mythologist Joseph Campbell spent his life research-ing common experiences that occur around the world, regardless of culture or time period. One of those experiences he called the Hero's Journey. He posited that when we are able to see our individual paths amid the backdrop of a universal journey, we shift our perspective and open ourselves up to personal transformation. He maintained there was a unique power in using symbols to chart our progress, or lack thereof. He claimed we each live our own myths, making us the heroes of our own journeys. If we distill the journey to its basic elements, we have: Departure (the hero leaves the familiar world behind); Initiation (the hero learns to navigate the unfamiliar world); and Return (the hero returns to the familiar world with expanded knowledge or horizon).

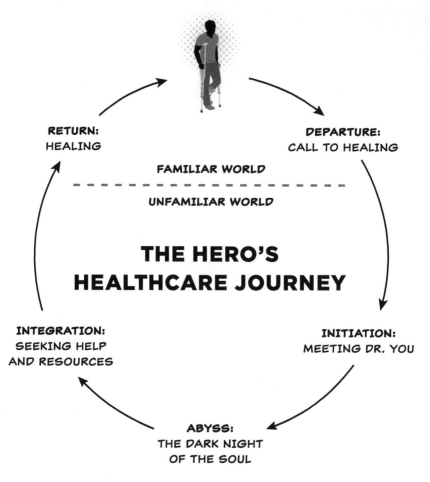

RETURN:
HEALING

DEPARTURE:
CALL TO HEALING

FAMILIAR WORLD

UNFAMILIAR WORLD

THE HERO'S HEALTHCARE JOURNEY

INTEGRATION:
SEEKING HELP
AND RESOURCES

INITIATION:
MEETING DR. YOU

ABYSS:
THE DARK NIGHT
OF THE SOUL

Using the journey set forth by Campbell, we can customize it to create the Hero's Healthcare Journey. Understanding the journey can help demystify the process and highlight the benefits inherent to the struggles. Campbell posits that the journey begins with a Call to Adventure, in which the hero must leave what she knows. Something in her circumstance pushes her off the ledge. In the case of healthcare, the Call to Healing begins when you have a physical accident or a health crisis, or when you receive a foreboding diagnosis. In this initial stage, your world is turned upside down. You may resist this initially; then eventually, something propels you and ultimately takes you past the point of no return. Your health condition, for example, might deteriorate to the point where you can no longer deny that something is going on, and you need to take steps to correct it.

At the onset of the journey, you—the hero—have no control over the situation. You must first begin your Healthcare Journey by heeding the call and entering a new, unfamiliar world. This might be finding yourself in the infusion center of a cancer clinic, a place you never identified with. It might be at the dialysis clinic amid people who heretofore seemed "foreign" to you. This can be an unnerving and ego-shattering experience. Your entire identity has shifted, and it takes some time and patience to fully accept the new totalities of your experience.

Luckily, you are not alone for long, because soon you meet your mentor—Dr. You. With your mentor by your side, you brave a series of thresholds, including the Dark Night of the Soul. Those who have been ill know this place well. It's desolate, it's lonely, it's dark. No one can reach you here. It's like living in an alternate realm. It seems far away from everyone you love, yet your journey to get there might occur overnight. It's important to note that once you have been in this emotional landscape, you can revisit it quite quickly. If you have finished your cancer treatments, for example, and months later have a sore neck that doesn't resolve, you could immediately find yourself panicked, overcome with grief and fear. There is a legitimate element of PTSD surrounding health crises. It's so easy to find yourself slipping back to the place you fought so hard to leave. Be patient and kind with yourself. Lean on Dr. You to set up appointments and any testing that might give you peace of mind about your health. The good news is that once you have been through the proverbial Dark Night of the Soul and survived, you know your way out. Though you might revisit in times of fear, you will never again doubt your reliance and strength to endure in the same way.

After what feels like an endless dark night, there is a dawning, a moment of realization. In the healthcare space, this is the stage of integration where you start seeking help. You begin your consultations with, for example, a physician. Or you start getting different opinions of physicians. You're on a quest for answers, so you start doing your own research. You become emboldened by your own knowledge. At this point, you have experienced the "belly of the whale," as Campbell calls it—in reference to the Bible story of Jonah being swallowed by the whale—and you have survived. After integration of this new empowerment, you are resurrected as a more evolved personality. Now, you reenter the familiar world having evolved and gown.

The Hero's Journey symbolizes how we face, confront, and overcome crises. Those can be crises of external nature or internal nature. The challenging thing about healthcare calamities is that they become both, which makes them more unique to deal with. When you're dealing with a physical ailment that often has impacts on your psychology, it can fundamentally reshape your human experience. It not only helps to redefine your relationship with the outside world, but it also forces you to rethink your relationship with yourself in a way very few other challenges can do. So many of us take our next breath for granted, our next heartbeat. People who are confronted by healthcare challenges are forced to confront the reality that the next heartbeat or next breath may never come, making the experience utterly terrifying. For somebody who has a heart condition, for example, a heart palpitation could evoke the sense of, *This is it.*

This vulnerability forces, accelerates, and exacerbates the cycle of the Hero's Journey.

To achieve true, deep, and lasting well-being, we must embark on the Hero's Healthcare Journey. We need to look within, be honest, and evaluate the causes of our health issue, if there are any. Sometimes there are not—as in congenital malformations, genetic precursors, accidents—but oftentimes, we know we weren't taking proactive, daily measures in support of optimal health. Sometimes even changes in personal beliefs and behaviors can have dramatic impacts on our well-being.

The journey we've outlined makes you a more discerning patient, health advocate, and even consumer. You are more knowledgeable and powerful, and you therefore hold your healthcare team to higher standards. Every encounter with people, stress, food makes you question the health impacts. Should you eat fats? Should you continue to stay at a job that you hate? Does this person, decision, or food help you heal yourself? Does it help you understand what's going on with your body? In chapter 7, we will look closer at changes you can make today to improve your health tomorrow.

The most powerful part of the Healthcare Hero's Journey is living with compromised health and not having answers. It is a humbling experience and can be extremely lonely and alienating. When you're dealing with big challenges like divorce and death in the family, others can relate because many have experience with them. When it comes to battling an invisible disease that is destroying your ability to walk, for example, people can't often relate. Or it's too hard to relate. So much of our identities is built around being able to perform—at our jobs, in our homes, with our kids. Healthcare crises can instantaneously make simple and mundane tasks, like getting groceries, into colossally challenging ordeals.

During these trials, however, you're not as alone as you think. Looking around, it's easy to assume that everybody is healthy and pain free, but you'd be surprised by how many people suffer daily pain. I do believe that with time, dedication, and sufficient focus and openness to the journey, we become bigger, better, and healthier in the end. This is why the Hero's Journey is a useful model in understanding that—just like the myth of magical pills—there is no shortcut through the journey. It's arduous and complicated, but it's a prerequisite to rebirth. There is no phoenix rising without the burning. As scary as the journey is, it's a sign that you really are going through a transformation. You are heading toward the outcome. If you continue along the same path, it's just a matter of time until you get there. After the fire and the journey, there is a treasure awaiting us—wholeness.

> THERE IS NO SHORTCUT THROUGH THE JOURNEY. IT'S ARDUOUS AND COMPLICATED, BUT IT'S A PREREQUISITE TO REBIRTH. THERE IS NO PHOENIX RISING WITHOUT THE BURNING.

The wholeness you discover is due to unearthing new aspects of your personality that are protective, empowered, and kind. You have found your inner guide—Dr. You. Once you find that guide, you realize it was there all along, but you've just become aware of yourself in a new way. Dr. You will never leave as long as you pay attention to that inner voice that communicates to you when it's overwhelmed, unwell, discomforted. Likewise, it calls your attention to happiness, confidence, validation. After your Hero's Healthcare Journey, it becomes a lot harder to get lost in that darkness, to be misled, and to lose faith in that final outcome. Dr. You is here to remind you not to accept the status quo. You deserve more, and to hell with everything that makes you accept less. Be your own hero. Fight back. Take the next step forward. This is your journey. It's time to begin.

EXAM NOTES:

⇨ The Call to Healing begins when you have a physical accident or a health crisis, or when you receive a foreboding diagnosis. In this initial stage, your world is turned upside down.

⇨ You are not alone for long, because soon you meet your mentor—Dr. You.

⇨ With your inner mentor by your side, you brave a series of thresholds, including the Dark Night of the Soul.

⇨ After what feels like an endless dark night, there is a dawning, a moment of realization. In the healthcare space, this is the stage of integration where you start seeking help and empowering yourself with answers.

⇨ After integration of this new empowerment, you are resurrected as a more evolved personality. Now, you reenter the familiar world having grown and become stronger and healthier than before.

6

——//——

CHAPTER 6:

OPTIMUM HEALTH
IS YOUR RIGHT

You can tell what a society values by tracking how its members spend their money. According to the Bureau of Economic Analysis, consumer spending makes up roughly 68 percent of the US economy.[32] The 2017 report from the Bureau of Labor Statistics (BLS) shows that the typical American household had an income of $75,573 before taxes, of which they spent an average of $60,060.[33] This was a 4.8 percent increase in spending from the previous year. So what are Americans spending money on? What is it we value? Some of the answers might surprise you.

Among other categories, the report shows that Americans annually spend $3,154 on eating out, $2,913 on entertainment, $787 on personal care products, $484 on alcoholic beverages, and $244 on beef. That's right—beef! Furthermore, Americans spend more than $1 billion on fireworks each year; if calculating by weight, that equals

---

32   Bureau of Economic Analysis, "Percent Change from Preceding Period in Real Gross Domestic Product," September 28, 2017, https://apps.bea.gov/scb/pdf/2017/10-October/1017-selected-nipa-tables.pdf.

33   Bureau of Labor Statistics, "Consumer Expenditures 2017," September 11, 2018, https://www.bls.gov/news.release/cesan.nr0.htm.

about 268 million pounds of fireworks—or, in starker terms, roughly a pound of fireworks for every American.[34] That's a lot of fireworks! Moreover, Americans bought more than $80 billion in lottery tickets in 2016.[35] These numbers show that Americans are not afraid of a good time, or of spending money on seemingly frivolous things. What the BLS report does not gauge, however, is how much money people spend on their health.

There's one thing you currently own, that you got for free, that is more valuable than all the fireworks and beef you could buy: your health. Health is free, but it can become quite expensive if you don't maintain it. The average American could live without a palatial home, a TV, daily Starbucks, maybe even a car—but you cannot live without your body and your health. It's time to check ourselves and our priorities. It's time to take ownership of our health.

As discussed, doctors and health industry practitioners have traditionally maintained a reactive response; self-advocacy, however, means taking a proactive stance. This means that in addition to taking Dr. You to all medical appointments and research sessions, Dr. You must be involved on a daily basis, ensuring that the small choices you make each day are aligned with your optimal health goals.

There are unlimited variations for what *optimal health* means. If you ask an athlete what 100 percent means to them on the average day, you will get a very different answer than if you ask an office worker who hasn't left her desk for the last three to four months. Based on quality of life and differing lifestyles, we all expect different things

---

34 "US Fireworks Industry Revenue Figures Breakdown by Industry Segment 1998–2017," American Pyrotechnics Association, https://www.americanpyro.com/assets/docs/FactsandFigures/Fireworks%20Revenue%20REV%206.22by%20Industry%20Segment%201998-17.pdf.

35 "Frequently Asked Questions," North American Association of State and Provincial Lotteries, http://www.naspl.org/faq.

from our health. For somebody who's extremely active, any level of pain or delay in treatment could be detrimental, not just physically but also emotionally and mentally. Other people want *any* semblance of their lives back, whether that's transitioning from a walker to a cane or simply being able to throw a ball with their child.

It's time to get to know your body by thinking about what your optimal health looks like. Some of you may have gotten accustomed to living and operating at 80 percent, 60 percent, even 20 percent of your capacity for well-being.

WHAT WOULD IT LOOK LIKE IF YOU WERE TO INCREASE YOUR QUALITY OF LIFE BY 5 PERCENT? MAYBE YOU'LL TAKE THAT EXTRA VACATION. MAYBE YOU'LL SLEEP BETTER. MAYBE YOU'LL HAVE LESS INFLAMMATION AND THEREFORE BE LESS LIKELY TO DEVELOP CHRONIC DISEASE.

_____

_____

_____

_____

IF YOU WERE TO WAKE UP TOMORROW FEELING 100 PERCENT, WHAT WOULD YOUR DAY CONSIST OF?

_____

_____

KNOWING WHAT YOUR OPTIMAL DAY WOULD LOOK LIKE (ABOVE), WHAT ARE THREE THINGS YOU WOULD LIKE TO BE HEALTHY ENOUGH TO ACHIEVE? FOR SOME, THAT MIGHT BE TO

RUN A MARATHON; FOR OTHERS, THAT MIGHT BE TO CHECK THE
MAILBOX UNASSISTED, TIE YOUR SHOES, OR TAKE THE DOG FOR
A WALK. BE HONEST WITH YOURSELF. DON'T COMPARE YOURSELF
TO OTHERS OR TO YOURSELF DECADES AGO.

1. _____

2. _____

3. _____

Take your answers with you on your next appointment with doctors, nutritionists, or coaches. Show them your responses, and tell them these are your daily, manageable goals. Ask them how you could make small changes today to add 5 percent to your overall health and well-being.

If you have ever tried a strict diet plan or an unrealistic training program, you know how detrimental these can be to your health. You must know yourself intimately so you can demand that your doctor treat you—not a patient, not a sufferer of a chronic disease, not a cash cow, but *you*. It's also important that Dr. You be there in case a doctor is dismissive or unhelpful. It's true that not all maladies have an immediate and exact diagnosis, but a doctor needs to have a plan in place to help diagnose your issue or send you someplace that can.

Often, when diagnoses become complex, physicians might question your mental health. They might say, "It's all in your head. It's psychological." If you are advocating for your child's mysterious symptoms, you might hear a doctor say that your child is faking it or vying for attention. For example, in 2014, a previously healthy seven-year-old girl was rushed to an Oregon hospital because she was experiencing sudden partial paralysis. Because the case was unusual and confounding, the rehabilitation expert at the children's hospital told the parents that their daughter was not really paralyzed; instead, he posited that the child was reacting emotionally to the birth of her baby sibling several months prior. He diagnosed her with a mental illness called conversion disorder. Her mother, like most parents, realized she had to advocate for her daughter. In an interview, she told reporters how she responded to the doctor: "I said, 'You've been with my child for 15 minutes, and you think it's psychological? Get out of my face.'"[36] The doctor then alluded to the mother being sleep deprived and unstable. Luckily the parents were very much in touch with Dr. You, and they continued to fight for their daughter and push for further testing. On an MRI, it was eventually discovered that the girl was suffering from acute flaccid myelitis (AFM), a disease similar to polio. After receiving a diagnosis, the child underwent the treatment and therapies she needed, and four years later, she could walk again.

I wish I could say this was an isolated case; but the truth is, it's not. There is no data to show how often doctors misdiagnose a physical illness as a psychological one, but almost everyone knows at least one person this has happened to. Dr. Allen Frances, former chair of psychiatry at the Duke University School of Medicine says, "Mental disorders become the default position to deal with medical uncertainty. It's widespread, and it's dangerous."[36] As we've discussed in previous chapters, doctors are human and therefore fallible. We can't expect all doctors to be expert diagnosticians, but we can hold them to a standard of care that allows for them to be honest about their uncertainties.

Dr. Mark Graber, president emeritus of the Society to Improve Diagnosis in Medicine claimed, "Physicians have an obligation to do a thorough workup before turning to a psychological explanation.

---

36   Elizabeth Cohen, "'Widespread and dangerous': Facing medical uncertainty, some doctors tell patients it's all in their heads," *CNN*, December 25, 2018.

When a doctor can't find a cause, that's a great time to get a second opinion or consult with a specialist."[36] Having Dr. You with you during these moments means that critical questions will be asked of the doctor to determine how confident they are in a diagnosis. Just as the mother of the girl with AFM displayed, it's OK to fight for your health and the health of your loved ones. In fact, there is nothing worth fighting for more.

MAKE SURE THAT YOUR DOCTOR'S METHODOLOGY MATCHES YOUR BELIEF SYSTEM. IF NOT, FIND A NEW DOCTOR.

One job of Dr. You is to make sure that your doctor's methodology matches your belief system. If not, find a new doctor. As many people know, however, finding a doctor can be quite tricky. Whether you are looking for one doctor, or a team of doctors, you must do your research first. Understand that even if you find a perfect match, your doctor will not be the best go-to for every issue, so always be prepared to find new ones.

Finding a doctor is not unlike finding a mate—there are awkward moments of getting to know each other. There are deep conversations about intimate matters; there are even times you're miffed by his seeming disinterest—not to mention that occasional disrobing! This is why you must learn to date your doctor, so you can find Dr. Right.

DATING YOUR DOCTOR

⇨ **DECIDE WHAT TYPE OF DOCTOR YOU WANT.** If you're unsure of what type of specialist to see, I recommend starting with a general practitioner or an internist to help you narrow your issue to one field (or more, if needed).

⇨ **DO YOUR RESEARCH.** Just as you wouldn't go on a first

date before conducting an internet search on the person (you know you would!), do the same for your doctors. Pay attention to when they were in school. Where are they from? Are they up to date on their training? What are their specialties? Can you find any information about their medical philosophy? Make sure you also look for patient reviews, which can offer valuable information on their personality and patient rapport.

☞ **BE PREPARED.** Make sure to take your entire medical file, including lists of all medicines and supplements that you take. Have a list of questions written out because invariably you might blank when it's time to ask. You might want to use some of the prompts listed below:

- *TELL ME ABOUT YOUR PHILOSOPHY ON HEALTH.*

- *TELL ME ABOUT YOUR BACKGROUND.*

- *WHAT ARE YOUR SPECIALTIES?*

- *WHAT'S YOUR TREATMENT PHILOSOPHY?*

- *WHAT'S YOUR EXPERIENCE WITH _____ (A SPECIFIC AREA THAT YOU MIGHT BE CONCERNED ABOUT)?*

- *BASED ON OUR CONVERSATION AND THE SYMPTOMS THAT I SHARED WITH YOU, WHAT DO YOU BELIEVE COULD BE HAPPENING OR COULD BE THE CAUSE OF MY ISSUE?*

  ° Listen to what they say. If they immediately jump to a conclusion, it's OK to doubt them because doctors make mistakes, and doctors also have biases. A doctor who is a proficient diagnostician usually will have a few things they need to eliminate before they arrive at the final conclusion. Also, be wary of the opposite as well. A physician who is reluctant to commit to any potential diagnosis or a strategic plan might be planning on conducting unnecessary tests that cost you valuable time and money.

- **HOW MUCH WILL IT COST? IS THIS THE MOST COST-EFFECTIVE WAY TO PROCEED?**

  - Don't leave the office with a stack of prescriptions or testing orders without confirmation of the costs. Oftentimes, physicians assume that you have insurance that will cover procedures and lab tests, which may or may not be the case. Make sure to get this clarification to save yourself the stress later.

- **WHAT DO YOU SEE AS THE NEXT STEP? HOW CAN WE WORK TOGETHER? HOW DO YOU SEE US WORKING TOGETHER MOVING FORWARD ON THIS?**

  - The right doctor will give you enough detail about what you might be able to expect without making big promises like, "I will have this figured out by your next visit. I know what's wrong with you. This is it, and you'll be out of here in no time." Don't accept this snake oil. Make sure their answer resonates with what you feel like a reasonable timeline would look like.

🖎 **ARE THEY RIGHT FOR YOU?** Don't ignore red flags. Does the doctor listen while you're talking? Are they dismissive? Rushing through the appointment? Do they ask for your questions and take the time to answer them thoroughly? Do they offer lifestyle and dietary changes, or do they go straight to prescribing pharmaceuticals?

▨⇨ **ARE THEY ESTABLISHING A CODEPENDENT RELATION-SHIP?** Do they have a plan to get you to your 100 percent, or are they wanting you to be reliant on them forever? Some of these could be early warning signs about their mindset in care. Some physicians look for a dependency in their patients, so patients become a recurring profit model for them. Usually the right kinds of physicians are the ones that don't want to see you that often because they want to actually get you to a healthy place. They measure their success by how happy and healthy you are.

▨⇨ **DON'T BE AFRAID TO GET MORE OPINIONS.** Just as you wouldn't marry someone after one date, don't be afraid to play the healthcare field. There are many fish in the sea, and with Dr. You by your side, you are bound to find a doctor who's right for you.

One of the reasons I developed the concept of dating your doctor is because I found myself in a patient-doctor relationship that was codependent. During my arduous quest for a diagnosis for my previously mentioned fatigue (that eventually led to the dog pills!), I met a doctor who diagnosed me with Lyme disease. I was immediately devastated. I was told, "Lyme is for life, and it can never be cured, and you'll always have to be managed." If I were to buy into that mentality, I wouldn't question it, and I would essentially be dependent on this physician for the rest of my life. This would mean I would be financially bound to her and her treatments as well. I looked at the lifetime of treatments ahead of me and realized it wasn't sustainable. I refused to accept this as my fate. As I began to do my own research, I realized I had not been given a positive diagnosis. In other words, nothing showed I had Lyme disease, but nothing showed I didn't. My lab tests had come back marginal, so the strategy my doctor was proposing was to treat me as if I had Lyme and see if my symptoms improved. Essentially, she was throwing mud at the wall. Since this time, I've talked to many people who share this experience. They spent way too much money in return for a dubious diagnosis that made them reliant on a doctor. It is my hope that in dating a doctor first, we can make more informed decisions on the people we put at the helm of our healing. May we find Dr. Right, who wants us to be independent leaders of our own health instead of dependent minions who rely on someone else's care.

> IT IS MY HOPE THAT IN DATING A DOCTOR FIRST, WE CAN MAKE MORE INFORMED DECISIONS ON THE PEOPLE WE PUT AT THE HELM OF OUR HEALING.

It is a luxury to have time to prep and plan before a doctor visit, because, as I knew too well, when a health crisis hits, you feel desperate. No matter how informed you are, there comes a point when you want so desperately to be "fixed" that you overlook some of the warning signs we've just mentioned. When that happens, forgive yourself. In my case, I got to a point where my mysterious health conditions were undeniable. I was exhausted, achy, weak, and not myself. I *knew* something was wrong, but no one could give me an answer. At one doctor visit, I was feeling particularly desperate for my optimal health. I was scared and concerned. I went in needing a solution. I remember looking at the doctor and saying, "Just do whatever tests you need to do." I ended up spending a lot of money on an initial round of tests. When I went in for my follow-up, excited to finally have an answer, the physician said, "I still don't know what's wrong with you because none of the results were conclusive.

We need to do more tests." I obliged and underwent more tests. At this point, I had spent thousands of dollars, but thought it would all be worth it when I returned for my third visit: I was ready for my insights, but they never came. The doctor said, "These tests aren't pointing in any direction. We need to order a few more tests." With a nudge from Dr. You I asked, "How much will it cost?" He said, "Well, this one is $2,000. This is $1,800. This is $3,200—" I interrupted, "Whoa, whoa, whoa. I don't have another $7,000 to spend on lab tests to figure out what's going on. There's got to be a better way to do this." He went on to explain that he could cut one panel out and send me to a different lab that takes longer but is much cheaper than the private lab in Germany he typically uses. What I realized is that I was paying extra to use his *preferred* vendors. The doctor may or may not have gotten a cut from the vendor, but I was certainly unnecessarily spending money. I have made these mistakes, and I don't want others to make them.

If you have been in this situation and spent your savings on healthcare, don't feel embarrassed. Even somebody like myself, who's in the healthcare space, can be vulnerable because when it comes to your health, fear, panic, and the desire to be well take over. This is a natural response to a crisis. This is why Dr. You will be with you, with a steady gaze and unflinching commitment to getting you to your optimal health. When you truly have a health crisis, you are at your weakest, most fearful state. It is in these moments that you must remember to manage your expectations. As a patient, don't go in thinking, *I'm going to take this test, and I'm going to know what's wrong with me*, because the instances of this happening are slim. It's usually a long game, so be prepared.

Furthermore, like many things, health issues tend to get worse before they get better. This might mean that your health issue that is related to one system has now affected another system. Do not lose hope when this happens; it's merely biology. Just like a leaky roof on the south side of a house can end up causing a leak on the north side of a house because of the way water flows, the cause-and-effect relationships in your body are very similar. Sometimes an issue of one system can manifest as a symptom in a totally different place.

For this reason, you need a doctor who will not be isolated to just one system. A physician who only believes a heart issue is in the heart is never going to be able to fully diagnose what's at the core of your problem. Instead, find Dr. Right, who can speak of your health and your organism in a holistic way. The physician who has the highest chance of resolving your issue is the one who understands that the body consists of many systems that need to operate together and well in order for you to achieve optimal health.

PERSONALIZED MEDICINE

Everyone knows how to enhance health—eat well, exercise, sleep well, detox. There are numerous books, blogs, and research around various health strategies. What isn't emphasized as much is how relevant wellness is. Enhancing your well-being is about personalized health solutions. This is what Dr. You excels in. It is easy to be bombarded by health plans—whether it's diet protocols, probiotic strains, certain mushrooms—and it's great to be aware of such a variety of methods. The danger, however, is that something that might make your friend lose weight and feel great might make you tired and bloated.

The future of medicine is about personalized solutions, or personalized medicine. (It is important to note, however, that though we will focus on the benefits of personalized medicine, they do not apply in all scenarios, as there are some proven standardized methods that offer great benefits.) Not every cure has the same results on every body. Not every diet leads to the same results. Not every combination of nutrition, exercise, and sleep will cause the same response in a specific organism. Dr. You's main responsibility in this context is finding your ideal chemistry. What is that perfect combination of factors that are custom tailored to you? Just like your clothes and your shoes need to fit you, so do your healthcare habits. That includes everything from the way you treat your muscles and your skin, to the way that you eat and the way that you go about every decision you make.

Personalized medicine has allowed many people to achieve their optimal states and has ushered in the concepts of body hacking, or biohacking. Ten years ago these concepts sounded like some obscure futuristic phenomenon, and in a way, they are. Previously we saw this concept in comic books and sci-fi movies where certain characters achieved superhuman breakthroughs. Biohacking and body hacking take the superhero experimentation and apply it to regular human beings. The way to get there? Personalized medicine.

People who were previously thought to be societal outliers have long since tried biohacking techniques. Many would travel to remote locations of the world and experiment by putting themselves on extreme diets or fasting regimens. Some might exclude dairy. Some might exclusively eat dairy. Some might use crystals to heal. Others might use isolation or even tobacco to heal. The concepts, though on the fringe of wellness, were created by early pioneers of personalized medicine because these individuals were taking their own body's needs and chemistry into account. They were using their unique bodies to experiment and derive some empirical data on healing. They were less inclined to care about what worked for others; instead, they were seeking personalized solutions to their health problems.

Many times, the strategies body hackers propose seem outlandish.

Consider author and entrepreneur Dave Asprey, who, after a visit to Tibet in 2004, became interested in the perceived mental benefits he experienced after consuming yak-butter tea. There was a time when the thought of adding full-fat butter to anything, especially a beverage, seemed preposterous. Only a decade later, however, Asprey founded Bulletproof 360 Inc., which has changed the way Americans take their coffee. Asprey himself has estimated that his recipe is responsible for 150 million cups of coffee, and his bottled versions are the highest-selling ready-to-drink coffees at Whole Foods. He has taken the concept of hacking his own body to new extremes, spending at least $1 million, by his estimate, on invasive stem cell procedures, hyperbaric oxygen chamber treatments, and infrared light sessions, in addition to the one hundred supplements he takes daily.[37]

Asprey's own journey with biohacking was a tumultuous one and began with a myriad of diagnoses including fibromyalgia, chronic Lyme disease, and Hashimoto's disease. Despite the diagnoses and subsequent treatments, he couldn't achieve his optimal health, so he began experimenting. He made himself a promise: "Every night after I finish work, I'm going to go home and … study. I'm going to troubleshoot this myself, because I am not getting help from the medical establishment. And I did that for four years. Every night, I would just study."[37] As he learned more about his own biology, he experienced a sense of empowerment, which fueled his interest in biohacking and has branded him a pioneer of human efficiency. He defines biohacking as the "science, biology, and self-experimentation to take control of and upgrade your body, your mind and your life" and also "the art and science of becoming superhuman."[37]

Although Asprey has a goal of living to 180, many people begin experimenting with biohacking for much humbler reasons—like getting rid of chronic pain, living another full year despite incurable cancer, or finding alternatives to major surgeries. Whatever the motivation, the goal is the same: empowerment and wellness. As we discussed in Chapter 4, being an active participant in your healthcare leads to better outcomes. Taking that a step further, as Asprey did, and immersing yourself in research, studies, and alternative therapies gives you a different perspective and can dispel the belief that you have no choice. Whether doctors have told you there is no choice, or you have just arrived at the conclusion after years of dead-end doctor visits, realizing there are options—even if they seem like new age fads—can offer hope.

Humans have always been curious about maximum human potential. We've always sought the miracle drug that can take us to the next level. The interesting thing about the biohacking trend of recent years is that it has less to do with that magic pill and more to do with nutrition, exercise, sleep, and emotional toxicity.

Thanks to the technological revolution, new devices and apps are available to allow for the monitoring of one's systems. These technologies have bridged the gap for consumers between themselves and diagnostic metrics without having to see a doctor. People start to wonder what else they can monitor about themselves, like tracking their sleep patterns or their menstrual cycle symptoms on mobile

---

37   Rachel Monroe, "The Bulletproof Coffee Founder Has Spent $1 Million in His Quest to Live to 180," *Men's Health,* January 23, 2019, https://www.menshealth.com/health/a25902826/bulletproof-dave-asprey-biohacking/.

apps. These technologies have normalized, and made it fun, to oversee personal metrics. People start to feel like they know their physiology in new ways that can have profound effects on how they seek care.

Furthermore, biohacking and related technologies have given us anecdotal knowledge that medications are not always the best route; instead, we build wellness on a foundation of healthy habits, diets, and lifestyles that take into account our own individual biology. This relatively small trend has the potential to manifest on a larger scale, affecting overall healthcare and treatment protocols.

The interest in mind, body, and spirit strategies ties to the evolution of popular tastes and culture. The 1990s and early 2000s particularly became an era of mass adoption of social media, digital news channels, and world news being replaced with local news. Suddenly, there was a personalization of the information that was being consumed. In the earlier stages of that trend, there was a period of time when mass media existed in a rather centralized fashion, and that allowed for the propagation of fairly stringent standards of aesthetics—for example, the idea that women should have certain proportions and look like supermodels, and men should have muscular dimensions and look like bodybuilders. For several years during this time, aesthetics became fairly extreme and removed from reality. This is really a generation-formative timeframe, where girls and boys were raised with the strange expectations about their bodies, and the bodies of their partners, and people around them. That also translated into this idea of unrealistically, exceptionally polished and superior beings, which became the goals for existence.

As time passed, we've shifted into a more fragmented media landscape. Suddenly, this supermassive and exaggerated ideal has been shattered, making room for a more personalized interpretation about what is "ideal." This is perhaps why there is more diversity and openness now around how to reach that ultimate potential; the answer is not to take a pill that makes you limitless. The answer is to explore what you need, learn about your own abilities and capacities, and ultimately find something that fits your lifestyle. What is your potential? What is your ideal? With the evolution of the media landscape and its shifting aesthetic norms, there's suddenly more room for personalized medicine and self-empowerment.

If you look at celebrities of today, they're no longer manufactured personalities like Britney Spears, the Spice Girls, and the Backstreet Boys. Instead, there are people who broadcast from their bedrooms. They might become Twitter celebrities overnight because they post a funny video of themselves dancing in the airport and get retweeted by famous comedians. This landscape gives voice to diversity in a way we haven't encountered before. Trends are no longer set by limited outlets; they're set by popular vote through "likes" and retweets. This has allowed people to question the long-set norms. Suddenly, women, for example, are questioning shaving their body hair, and when they question it, they can immediately find large groups online and join a campaign that supports that choice. Even though the biases are still deeply ingrained from decades of rigorous standards, it's exciting to see a growing pressure and drive to reconnect with some of the more humane and natural parts of ourselves.

REDEFINING OUR STANDARDS FOR WELL-BEING

As a culture, we spend so much time, energy, and money on the pursuit of happiness. It's the same quest as searching for the magic pill, diet, or shortcut to optimal health. We are always seeking that perfect job, that perfect relationship, that highly idealized, unrealistic goal that we set for ourselves. We've been doing this to our bodies, our minds, and our careers, and it's damaging our health and vitality.

When we set these unreachable standards, we are setting ourselves up to fail. So let's be honest and manage our expectations. Truthfully, we don't all need to wake up every morning feeling like we can rule the world. That's not realistic or sustainable. In the same way, we can enjoy our lives more by redefining our standards for well-being. When we have those days of boundless energy, we can appreciate them. When we don't have those days, we can still be joyful, engaged participants in our lives. We're not "less than" because we don't drink green shakes every meal and do yoga each day. There is a spectrum of health, and much of it has little to do with the physical body.

Well-being is about learning how to be happy and healthy every single day. Naturally, over time, you make decisions in your professional and personal lives that reflect this quest for joy. Many people think that if they had their ideal job, *then* they would be happy and healthy. Truthfully, however, I've seen people working at car washes who have found joy. When I drive away, I have a smile on my face because their happiness is contagious. Their fulfillment has little to do with their bodies and more to do with their minds. When we detach our happiness from our physical health, we are not as devastated by health challenges that inevitably arise with age.

Truly taking care of ourselves means finding joy in the tasks we're doing—whatever they are. It's not a goal for the future; it's happening now. When we are vessels of this kind of joy and happiness, we are less likely to buy into the myths that we should look a certain way or hold certain jobs. Optimal health is about being happy in your body and being happy in your life. Accept things as they are, and don't punish yourself by self-limiting standards.

The body you have been given, no matter its shape or size, is the most amazing and precious piece of equipment you will ever own, so arm yourself with the knowledge and skills to take the best care of it. The person who cares most about your health is you, so take ownership of your health, get informed, be passionate about well-being, and rethink your dependency on outdated systems and processes.

Optimal health is not something you think about on the day you go to the doctor. It's instead a practice, a discipline. It's hourly, minute-to-minute decisions—*Do I take the stairs or elevator? Do I have the sandwich or the vegetable plate? Do I buy the makeup with parabens or without?* The good news is the more we train ourselves to make these decisions, the more they become second nature. Initially it may be a challenge to transition to a new lifestyle, but once you pass this period, you will begin to find comfort in and even crave your new diet, exercise regimen, or style because it has become your new normal.

Every decision you make with your body is connected to your optimum health. And let's not forget the decisions you make with your wallet. As we've mentioned, Americans are master consumers. We vote with every purchase that we make. Whatever we spend our money on—whether it's cosmetics, cars, fireworks, or beef—we make informed choices that let corporations know that we are discerning consumers who have our optimal health in mind. In this, we can hold companies and regulatory bodies accountable. When we take this same discernment into our doctors' offices, we are casting votes about what we will and will not accept.

Healthcare crises can seem to remove one's choices, but it is only a façade. Take Dr. You with you to the beauty counter. Take Dr. You with you to the grocery store. Use these opportunities to create a standard and mission of optimal health and wholeness. Starting today, demand and expect a better level of care and quality of life because it is not just a luxury—it's an innate right.

EXAM NOTES:

⇨ In addition to taking Dr. You to all medical appointments and research sessions, Dr. You must be involved on a daily basis, ensuring that the small choices you make each day are aligned with your optimal health goals.

⇨ There are unlimited variations for what optimal health means.

⇨ Another job of Dr. You is to make sure that your doctor's methodology matches your belief system.

⇨ Truly taking care of ourselves means finding joy in the tasks we're doing—whatever they are. It's not a goal for the future; it's happening now.

⇨ Optimal health is not something you think about on the day you go to the doctor. It's instead a practice, a discipline.

7

CHAPTER 7:

THE GOLDEN EXCUSES

When my mother was diagnosed with breast cancer, we had numerous discussions of surgical options and treatment plans. I shared with her the many studies I'd read touting lifestyle and dietary measures that can positively impact a patient's recovery and recurrence risk. I told her to prepare herself for some big lifestyle and nutritional changes. She agreed fully and declared that she would be altering her diet completely. Several months after her treatments ended, I noticed many of the positive modifications she had made were disappearing. I heard her say things like, "Your father doesn't want to change his diet, so it's just easier this way." Other times, she declared, "I just like what I like!" Despite defying logic, my mother's response to change is quite common—once we feel good, we have a tendency to return to our old routines. We forget why we had the desire to change in the first place.

It is rational to assume that a person would change in the face of a health issue, but scores of research has shown otherwise. Dr. Edward Miller, retired dean of the medical school at Johns Hopkins University, was a trained anesthesiologist who specialized in drug effects on cardiovascular health. In one of his presentations, he discussed his work with patients whose heart disease was so severe they underwent bypass and/or angioplasties. About 600,000 people have bypasses every year in the United States, and each procedure can cost more than $100,000; adding the 1.3 million heart patients who have angioplasties annually, these procedures cost around $30 billion each year.[38] As Dr. Miller reported, the procedures do relieve chest pains temporarily but rarely prevent heart attacks or prolong lives. Luckily, many patients can avoid repeat surgeries by adopting healthier lifestyles. Yet very few do. "If you look at people after coronary-artery bypass grafting two years later, 90 percent of them have not changed their lifestyle," Miller said. "And that's been studied over and over and over again … Even though they know they have a very bad disease and they know they should change their lifestyle, for whatever reason, they can't."[38]

Why would we Americans rather undergo numerous costly and invasive surgeries than clean up our diets, stop smoking, exercise regularly, and manage stress? Why is it so common to suspend rational thinking just to avoid change? Before we get into specific action items to include in our Wellness Game Plan in the next chapter, let's first dispel the myths surrounding change so that we can remove any objections that might be barriers to our own well-being.

I call these common barriers the "golden excuses" because people feel so validated when they spit one of them out, like it's the end of the conversation. Period. At some point, however, we each have to confront our own failure to address our well-being. There is just no way around it. In order to help us do this, the following section is divided into three parts: first, we will learn about each of the golden excuses; second, we will hear Dr. You's succinct rebuttal; and third, we will participate in a "how to" item that helps us overcome relying on the excuse in the future.

---

38 Alan Deutschman, *Change or Die: The Three Keys to Change at Work and in Life* (New York: HarperBusiness, 2007), 3–4.

EXCUSE 1: CHANGE IS SCARY.

Change puts us in contact with the unfamiliar, and some people avoid this interaction at all costs. History shows that even our major world religions were formed to ease our anxieties about the unknown. *What is the loud booming in the skies? Must be an angry deity displeased with our recent actions!* Understandably, fear of the unknown is in our biology, but facing it can lead to greater evolution of our species. Despite the trepidation you might feel about a new routine, a revised grocery list, a different exercise regimen, the scarier alternative to change is bad health or reduced life expectancy. What is truly terrifying is dying early because you did not make a change. If fear or discomfort is your excuse for not making changes, you are not focusing on the priority, which is staying healthy and alive.

Since uncertainty is so frightening to some people, let's focus on what is certain: if you do not take care of something, you will have problems. It is certain that if you don't maintain your roof, for example, you will get leaks. You will get full gutters and potential flood damage. This cause-and-effect relationship is certain; what isn't certain is how bad the damage will be. Make changes today to ensure you're here tomorrow.

FOOD FOR THOUGHT FROM DR. YOU: What's worse than getting worse? There is a price to inaction, so if you feel fear, lean into it. Let your discomfort become a powerful motivator to embrace change.

HOW TO: In an entrepreneurial setting, I would tell people that if something scares you, go do it! In healthcare, however, I wouldn't necessarily give that same advice. Don't just lean into fear; lean into intuition, into what you know. Listen to that inner voice that's trying to tell you something. Maybe it's saying that something is wrong with your health. Maybe it's telling you that everything is OK. Other times, it might be telling you that your body needs attention. Or maybe it's urging you to take a step back and to stop trying to find a problem where there may be none. Since the messages are unique to the individual and the circumstances, it's important to access your intuition and begin to pay closer attention to it. Use this simple affirmation daily to check in with your body and stay engaged in the present moment:

IT IS A NORMAL EMOTION THAT IS SIMPLY HERE TO PROTECT ME AND GUIDE ME TO A BETTER LIFE.

I INTUITIVELY KNOW THAT I NEED TO CONSIDER _____ _____ (INSERT CHANGE/ACTION) FOR MY HIGHEST GOOD.

I NOW RELEASE MY _____ (INSERT EMOTION) AND EMBRACE TAKING THIS ACTION.

EXCUSE 2: I CAN'T AFFORD THE FOOD/EXERCISE/ TIME NEEDED TO MAINTAIN GOOD HEALTH.

Chronic diseases, such as heart disease, cancer, and diabetes, are responsible for seven of every ten deaths in America annually. These chronic diseases are largely preventable by eating healthy, exercising regularly, avoiding tobacco, and receiving preventive services and screenings. Reactive treatments for diseases account for 75 percent of the nation's health spending.[39] Proactive health maintenance not only prevents disease but also keeps people in the early stages of disease from getting sicker. Preventing disease not only keeps healthcare costs down, but it is also the key to helping people live longer, healthier lives.

---

39 "Preventative Healthcare," Centers for Disease Control and Prevention, last modified September 15, 2017, https://www.cdc.gov/healthcommunication/ toolstemplates/entertainmented/tips/PreventiveHealth.html.

FOOD FOR THOUGHT FROM DR. YOU: You can cut down-stream costs for care if you invest in maintaining your health and monitor wellness regularly to diagnose conditions early. Not making health changes can cost you dearly—the ultimate price being your life.

HOW TO: Let's make this super simple and check the price tag on your health. Take one thing in your life that you know is not good for your health that you're doing anyway (drinking, smoking, excessive caffeine consumption, etc.). Use the formula below to determine how much you spend on this activity. After you have calculated the lifetime amount of money you will spend on your chosen activity, research the health effects most linked to that activity. To use our below example of smoking, how much money do lung cancer surgeries and treatments cost on average? What about the income you'd lose from not being able to work or take care of your household? Add this amount to the amount you spend on a bad habit in a lifetime. Guaranteed, this total will shock you and will be far more expensive than what you could pay now for a gym membership, organic fruits and vegetables, meditation classes, or anything to help counter the negative effect. The math shows, it's way more expensive to be sick than to be healthy. Ask the 20 percent of Americans who find themselves burdened by substantial medical debt.[40] I wonder how their choices might be different if they could do it over again? *Example: Smoking.* Let's say you are forty years old and smoke a pack of cigarettes a day, with the average pack in the United States costing $5.50 (though in places like California, it's over $10).

---

40 Carlos Dobkin, Amy Finkelstein, Raymond Kluender, and Matthew J. Noto-widigdo, "Myth and Measurement: The Case of Medical Bankruptcies," *New England Journal of Medicine* (March 2018). https://www.ncbi.nlm.nih.gov/pmc/articles/PMC5865642/.

$$\$5.50 \text{ DAILY COST OF SMOKING}$$
$$\times \quad 365 \text{ DAYS A YEAR}$$
$$= \$2007.50 \text{ YEARLY COST}$$

$$78 \text{ AVERAGE LIFE SPAN}$$
$$- \quad 40 \text{ DAYS A YEAR}$$
$$= \quad 38 \text{ YEARS LEFT}$$

$$38 \text{ YEARS LEFT}$$
$$\times \ \$2007.50 \text{ YEARLY COST OF SMOKING}$$
$$= \$76,285 \text{ AMOUNT YOU WILL SPEND IN A LIFETIME ON SMOKING}$$

$$\$76,285 \text{ AMOUNT YOU WILL SPEND IN A LIFETIME ON SMOKING}$$
$$+ \$75,000 \text{ AVERAGE COST OF TREATMENT FOR LUNG CANCER}$$

$151,285

AMOUNT OF MONEY YOU HAVE ACTIVELY SPENT
TO COMPROMISE YOUR HEALTH AND THE AMOUNT
OF MONEY YOU COULD SAVE OVER YOUR LIFETIME
BY STOPPING SMOKING TODAY.

Now that's a lot of money, isn't it? What else could you do with it if you had it on hand today? Perhaps a few better options are starting to crystalize in your mind here. So if you don't want to spend that amount of money, it's time to start thinking about making some different choices now. Rather than spend your wealth actively harming your health, change your choices, and make sure your hard-earned cash is going toward a healthier, happier, and ... richer you.

Here is a blank spreadsheet to do your own math:

NAME OF BAD HABIT/ACTIVITY _____

$ _____ DAILY COST OF ACTIVITY

× **365** DAYS A YEAR

= $ _____ YEARLY COST

78 AVERAGE LIFE SPAN

− _____ YOUR AGE

= _____ YEARS LEFT

_____ YEARS LEFT

× $ _____ YEARLY COST OF ACTIVITY

= $ _____ AMOUNT YOU WILL SPEND
IN A LIFETIME ON ACTIVITY

$ _____ AMOUNT YOU WILL SPEND
IN A LIFETIME ON ACTIVITY

+ $ _____ AVERAGE COST OF TREATMENT
FOR ACTIVITY

$ _____

AMOUNT OF MONEY YOU HAVE ACTIVELY SPENT
TO COMPROMISE YOUR HEALTH AND THE AMOUNT
OF MONEY YOU COULD SAVE OVER YOUR LIFETIME
BY STOPPING ACTIVITY TODAY.

EXCUSE 3: I DON'T HAVE ENOUGH SUPPORT.

We can all use our loved ones as excuses for stagnancy—_I may want to change, but my spouse is not going to change. It's going to be hard for me to convince my children to change_, and so on and so on. As we discussed, there is no knight in shining armor, no miracle or special hall pass from the natural laws of the universe coming to save you. When it comes to your health, you have to be self-centered. Whether there is support or not, your life choices and the changes you choose to make are all up to ... well, *you*! You have to be your advocate and put in the work. You can't rely on other people to get you well, exercise for you, or manage your actions day in and out. I know that sounds harsh; it is natural to want to lean in on a friend, a family member, or an expert. Being self-centered or selfish also has such negative connotations, but it is better than the alternative. When you struggle with health issues, you can become a very expensive burden, not just for yourself but for everybody else in your life. What is selfish is allowing it to get to that point without taking steps earlier to live in your best health.

Nobody else is responsible for your well-being but you. While it is good to have a support system, you don't necessarily need to start with one. In fact, as I've seen in my own life, once you start making better choices for yourself, the people in your life oftentimes follow suit. This can be a wonderful by-product of maintaining your own health. In the book *Connected*, authors Nicholas Christakis and James Fowler found that the behaviors of those around us have a direct, albeit subconscious, link to our own decisions. Their research showed that during a meal, "people randomly assigned to be seated near strangers who eat a lot wind up doing the same."[41] After studying this correlation, they determined that "our health depends on our own choices and actions, but it also depends on the choices and actions of those around us."[41]

Shortly after my grandma's passing, I convinced my mother—who

---

41 Nicholas Christakis and James Fowler, *Connected: The Surprising Power of Our Social Networks and How They Shape Our Lives* (New York: Little, Brown and Company, 2009), 106, 129.

was recovering from her cancer treatment—to take a trip with me to Venice. It was an opportunity to spend quality time together, celebrate our relationship, and honor my grandmother by doing something she'd always encouraged us to do: travel. Over a beautiful meal together that week, my mother commented offhandedly, "It's interesting that when I spend time with you, I eat so much more fish." I responded, "It's true; you do." I understood that my choices were affecting her choices, which was something countless hours of conversations about health data and cancer research had failed to do. It's like the cogs in a clock; when one starts turning in the opposite direction, all of them respond accordingly. Surrounded by centuries of Venice's history, we saw a clear path forward to change and a better, healthier tomorrow.

An uncomfortable reality is that if you aren't taking care of yourself when you're well because you lack support, that won't change when you become ill. Oftentimes people maintain a myth that someone will show up and support them when they get sick. I'm sorry to say, that rarely happens. In fact, that is when people typically scurry away. If people are not there for you when you're healthy, they are likely not going to be there for you when you're not. Unfortunately, this reality cannot be transformed overnight, but you can still change yourself. When you have the courage to confront change, you will see the people around you following suit. In that way, new people might show up in support of you who weren't there before.

> **FOOD FOR THOUGHT FROM DR. YOU:** Dr. You is always there, advocating for your well-being. Integrating Dr. You into your current and future care plans allows you to shift from dependence to independence.
>
> **HOW TO:** Ultimately, nobody can care for your health and well-being better than you. Even though the idea of being

alone is a scary one, embracing this notion can transition you from dependence to independence. When you are your own advocate, you are never really alone. For as long as there's you, there's a chance.

I want to share with you a simple mental exercise that was groundbreaking for me while I was working on my recovery. All you need is a mirror and a few minutes of your time.

Take a moment to turn off your phone to avoid interruption. Stand in front of a mirror. Now, turn your attention to yourself. Look at yourself in the mirror like you would your closest friend or partner. Next, while looking yourself in the eyes, say the statement below, and really mean it. I know it feels weird, but as I've learned from experience, there is great power in visualization. To be honest, when I tried this for the first time, I broke down in tears. I'd always thought I loved myself until I did this exercise and realized all I really saw were my flaws—my wrinkles, the anxiety in my eyes. It might be hard, but that's OK. You may really struggle with it, as I did, but keep doing it until you start to believe it and the exercise comes easily. In doing this, you will create empathy and love for yourself. This truly has the capacity to change lives and can redefine your relationship with people and yourself. Do this exercise once a day or as needed when you feel unsupported.

"(Your Name), I love you. I care about you. I am here for you always."

This exercise is designed to help you trust yourself more but also remain open to support systems as they present themselves, whether that is an individual, a support group, a hobby group, an online forum, or a hotline. Everyone has moments (sometimes lasting an hour, a week, a year) when they feel alone. Sometimes loneliness is simply an illusion. When was the last time you were on the street and looked around to find there was nobody there? It rarely happens. You're always surrounded by people, and sometimes when we perceive ourselves as lonely, we just need to take action to connect with another human, even if that's a conversation about the weather with a grocery clerk. In fact, research by University of British Columbia psychologist Elizabeth Dunn and her colleague Gillian M. Sandstrom showed that even trivial conversations with people we run into randomly—which they termed "weak ties"—have the power to transform feelings of connectedness and happiness, "suggesting that even social interactions with the more peripheral members of our social networks contribute to our well-being."[42] Look for these moments of connection and engage in them, no matter how seemingly insignificant. They can save your health and your life.

EXCUSE 4: I'M TOO YOUNG/HEALTHY/ABLE-BODIED TO WORRY ABOUT THIS NOW.

When the National Cancer Institute recently reported that even one alcoholic beverage a day increases your risk of cancers of the oral cavity and pharynx, esophagus, and female breast, I polled my friends' reactions.[43] Considering most of my friends are in their thirties and forties, I was curious what their responses would be. Almost every one of them said some variant of, "I'm too young to need to worry about

---

42   Gillian M. Sandstrom and Elizabeth Dunn, "Social Interactions and Well-Being: The Surprising Power of Weak Ties," *Personality and Social Psychology Bulletin* 40, no. 7 (July 1, 2014): 910–922. https://doi.org/10.1177/0146167214529799.

43   "Alcohol and Cancer Risk," National Cancer Institute, last modified September 13, 2018, https://www.cancer.gov/about-cancer/causes-prevention/risk/alcohol/alcohol-fact-sheet.

that. That won't happen to me." This surprised me because just because you may *feel* invincible doesn't mean you *are* invincible. I know from personal experience that everyone feels this way until the moment they have evidence to the contrary. This has been the most challenging aspect of my healthcare journey over the last several years: accepting my own vulnerabilities and mortality. No matter how great I may feel today, I am not guaranteed tomorrow. This is a universal, archetypal lesson you don't know until you *know*, and then there's no going back.

I went through a crisis of sorts when I was faced with my own mortality. Ultimately, I accepted that I can't take anything for granted—not my physical well-being, but also not my mental well-being. As soon as I overcame my fear of death (to the extent that I could), then another fear came up, which was even harder for me—the fear of losing my mind. I went through a phase of questioning my sanity. When driving my car, I'd be overcome with worry about what would happen if I suddenly forgot how to drive. I think this myth of invincibility is the trickiest one to dispel. For me, there was nothing someone could have said or done to convince me otherwise. I needed to experience the fear of losing my physical and mental faculties so I could get to a place of gratitude, peace, acceptance, and celebration of life.

I was a smoker for many years. I tried to stop, but it never stuck for long. Around the same time I was trying to quit, I started doing some work based on self-love. My initial self-love "practice" was to look at myself in the mirror and say, "Lora, I love you," much like the exercise I outlined before. The real goal here was to say this phrase to myself the way I'd always wanted to hear it from parents, partners, friends. As I mentioned, it was hard for me at first. Really hard. In fact, I tried for over an hour and just could not bring myself to say it. Then I had to say it over fifty times before one of them rang true. Then tears ran down my cheeks. I was overwhelmed by sympathy for the woman looking at me in the mirror. I wanted to hug her, protect her, let her know she'd be OK. I thought, *Why was it so hard for me to say this and to mean it?* This small exercise made me aware that I didn't know how to love myself. I knew I couldn't expect anybody else to love me in that way if I couldn't do it myself. Do you truly believe you're lovable if you cannot love yourself? I realized suddenly all the ways this was manifesting in my personal life and intimate relationships.

Then I started thinking about some of these other choices in my life. I recognized that if I really loved myself, I wouldn't be smoking. Not only because I might develop cancer, but also because even if I don't develop cancer, it certainly was limiting my lung capacity. It was destroying my skin. It was making me age faster. It was destroying my teeth. It was making it harder for me to breathe while running and hiking. The truth was that it altered how much enjoyment I could get from my life. When I acknowledged the hard truth that I was smoking because I didn't believe I was lovable, I suddenly saw my actions as self-destructive behavior. This was the critical moment when I was able to see my smoking habit for what it truly was, and I was then able to alter my choices.

Oftentimes, we harm ourselves through small, daily choices that are unconscious but insidious. If you love yourself and your life, why would you cause yourself to live with a third of the capacity of your lungs? Why would you choose to live with headaches? Why would you contribute to muscular atrophy? Organ dysfunction? Obviously the list goes on and on. These unconscious connections are vital to understanding ourselves and the role our daily choices make in our overall physical, mental, and spiritual health. Choosing to smoke, for example, is not just harming your health, but it might also be a by-product of a complicated relationship you have with yourself.

Hopefully people functioning under the myth of "It won't happen to me" are right. Maybe they won't experience a disease, but you might experience compromised quality of life, intimate relationships, and self-love. From a holistic wellness perspective, these compromises are the worst-case scenarios. We all know we will die; it happens to people of all ages every day. What is notable, however, is the number of deaths in individuals under age fifty. In 2017, for example, there were fifty-six million deaths globally; 24 percent were in those younger than forty-nine years old.[44] Don't you care about the time you're going to spend between now and then? If it is inevitable that it will happen to you, then why not make the best of life now? I understand that we can't all be perfect, and this is not intended to be a guide to perfection, but we can all be better by making better choices.

FOOD FOR THOUGHT FROM DR. YOU: Maybe you are right. Maybe you won't get a disease, not today, not this year. But are you living life like you love it? Let Dr. You guide you on a journey toward self-love, self-care, and better decision-making.

HOW TO: Have you ever been in a car accident? Have you ever had the flu? Have you ever lost your keys? You probably didn't think these would happen to you, but they did. The fact of life is we all lose our keys at least once (a day, for some of us): we all probably get the flu at least once; we all get into a car accident, small or big, at some point in our lives. Can we really deny that this is something that doesn't apply to the rest of our lives? The truth is, things happen, and no one is invincible. Life comes at you fast. Be prepared by keeping Dr. You close by for support and guidance.

---

44 Hannah Ritchie and Max Roser, "Causes of Death," *Our World in Data*, February 2018, https://ourworldindata.org/causes-of-death.

WHAT ARE THREE THINGS IN YOUR LIFE THAT HAVE TAKEN YOU BY COMPLETE SURPRISE?

1. _____

2. _____

3. _____

Now that you have your list, ask yourself if any of these could have been prevented or made better by self-love.

EXCUSE 5: I WILL CHANGE TOMORROW.

The myth of time is also a common myth we all buy into. The truth is, there's only one point in time that really exists. There's no past, there's no future, there's only today. Living with the idea that you will be happy *one day* is a sure way to never achieve it. When we live for *one day*, we might lose the only day that matters: today. The brutal truth is that you may not make it to *one day*. You may never land that promotion. You may never have enough money to buy your own house. You may never take that cruise. The idea that you cannot be happy and healthy *now* seems reckless and wasteful.

We've all heard the adage that when you are faced with death, your life flashes before your eyes. That's a selective truth. It's not like a montage from the '80s plays before you showing all your laughter and love. In fact, I think it's the opposite: I think in that moment, we see all the potential laughter we could have had instead of nights spent checking email or working like a dog. I think after these potentialities flash before us, we might all think, *I was such an idiot!* When we dispel this myth of boundless time, we are more present in our bodies, our relationships, and our lives. I find that I tell people I love them more often than I used to or I go snowboarding rather than waiting for some magic objective to be obtained. This is not a life overhaul. This is about doing the simple things that make you happy now.

> **FOOD FOR THOUGHT FROM DR. YOU:** The future is not your friend, but the present moment is. Acknowledge it and embrace it fully; it is the only time you will ever have with certainty.
>
> **HOW TO:** Let's spend the next five minutes finding out where you spend most of your time—past, present, or future. Clear your mind for a minute and focus on your breathing, and let's see what kind of a time traveler you are!
>
> Then, with your breathing slowed and your attention on your thoughts, write down the next ten thoughts you have. Literally whatever ideas pop up without filtering. Don't think about it too much; just jot down whatever thoughts pass through your mind.

1. _____

2. _____

3. _____

4. _____

5. _____

6. _____

7. _____

8. _____

9. _____

10. _____

When you have all of your previous ten thoughts recorded, look at each one individually, and determine whether that thought is about something that happened in the past, is happening at this exact moment, or will happen in the future, even if it's five minutes from now. Check the box below that corresponds with the answers you wrote above. Then total the numbers for each column to determine if you live mostly in the past, present, or future.

1. PAST_____ PRESENT _____ FUTURE_____

2. PAST_____ PRESENT _____ FUTURE_____

3. PAST_____ PRESENT _____ FUTURE_____

4. PAST_____ PRESENT _____ FUTURE_____

5. PAST_____ PRESENT _____ FUTURE_____

6. PAST_____ PRESENT _____ FUTURE_____

7. PAST_____ PRESENT _____ FUTURE_____

8. PAST_____ PRESENT _____ FUTURE_____

9. PAST_____ PRESENT _____ FUTURE_____

10. PAST_____ PRESENT _____ FUTURE_____

TOTALS: PAST_____ PRESENT _____ FUTURE_____

If your score above shows that you live mostly in the past, set a time for fifteen minutes each day journaling about your past experiences. How have they shaped your present moment? Consciously giving your brain time to travel to the past will allow the majority of your awareness to return to the present moment.

Similarly, if your scores show you spend most of your time in the future, set a fifteen-minute timer each day to give yourself time to list your goals, to-dos, worries, etc. How are they distracting you or affecting your present? Giving your mind time and conscious space to spend in the future will allow you greater mental freedom to remain in the present moment.

If your scores show that you live in the present, then congratulations. Continue being an engaged participant in your day, and share your skill with others.

This exercise allows you to slow your frenetic mind and focus your awareness on the now. Do this exercise regularly so you can check in with your time-traveling mind. With practice, you will notice you are training your brain to stay in the moment, and when your thoughts stray, gently remind yourself to stay in the now.

EXCUSE 6: I DON'T KNOW ENOUGH TO DECIDE WHICH CHANGES TO MAKE.

When you are suddenly faced with a health dilemma, there are many decisions to make. What medicine will you take? Will you choose surgical interventions? Will you begin a grain-free diet, vegetarian, Paleo, keto? You can see why people become paralyzed in the face of all these potential changes. People who have trouble making decisions are also motivated by a fear of regret. What if they make the wrong decision? What if, after a breast cancer diagnosis, for example, they take a medication that lowers their local recurrence risk but increases their risk of uterine cancer? It is difficult to make authentic decisions and life changes in these moments, and the person can become paralyzed by choice.

This excuse about choices has two sides: firstly, you can have too many choices, and secondly, you may feel you have no choice. Either way, the root of the fear is the same: regret. Will you regret doing *something?* Will you miss out on a better opportunity? Will you regret doing *nothing?* Psychologists have long warned us of decision fatigue, the state of low mental energy after making numerous decisions. In fact, the more choices you make in a single day, the harder it is for your brain to arrive at a decision. Psychologist Kathleen Vohs has done extensive research on how decision-making can deplete the brain's executive resources, which are responsible for focusing on specific tasks. Her research found that "making choices led to reduced self-control (i.e., less physical stamina, reduced persistence in the face of failure, more procrastination, and less quality and quantity of arithmetic calculations)."[45] Using this research, it's clear why many people see the myriad of diet protocols or exercise regimens and just shut down.

Author John Tierney notes that, as an effect of decision fatigue, the human brain will look for shortcuts in one of two ways: "One shortcut is to become reckless: to act impulsively instead of expending the energy to first think through the consequences. (Sure, tweet that photo! What could go wrong?) The other shortcut is the ultimate energy saver: do nothing."[46] If the brain does use these shortcuts when its executive function is depleted, it is easier to understand why it's hard to exercise after a long work day or why our dinner choices are sometimes less healthy than our breakfast choices. If we know that

---

45   K. D. Vohs, R. F. Baumeister, B. J. Schmeichel, J. M. Twenge, N. M. Nelson, D. M. Tice. "Making choices impairs subsequent self-control: a limited-resource account of decision making, self-regulation, and active initiative," *Journal of Personality and Social Psychology* (May 2008): 883–898. https://www.ncbi.nlm.nih.gov/pubmed/18444745?ordinalpos=2&itool=En trezSystem2.PEntrez.Pubmed.Pubmed_ResultsPanel.Pubmed_RVDocSum.

46   John Tierney, "Do You Suffer From Decision Fatigue?" *The New York Times Magazine* (August 2011). https://www.nytimes.com/2011/08/21/magazine/do-you-suffer-from-decision-fatigue.html.

we tend to make worse personal choices after many decisions, then maybe we do our grocery shopping in the morning. Maybe we make a weekly exercise plan on Sunday mornings. Maybe we show more mental discipline at the end of a long day and order steamed vegetables for dinner rather than burgers and fries.

Hopefully understanding decision fatigue can lead to sharper decision-making. Psychologist Barry Schwartz hopes that the growing number of choices in our culture will motivate us to become choosers rather than pickers. Pickers choose from what's available and hope for the best. Choosers, however, are thoughtful and discerning:

> A chooser is someone who thinks actively about the possibilities before making a decision. A chooser reflects on what's important to him or her in life, what's important about this particular decision, and what the short- and long-range consequences of the decision may be. A chooser makes decisions in a way that reflects awareness about what a given choice means to him or her as a person. Finally, a chooser is thoughtful enough to conclude that perhaps none of the available alternatives are satisfactory, and that if he or she wants the right alternative, he or she may have to create it.[47]

Whether you feel you have too many choices or too few, either one can paralyze you.

Both sides, however, are rooted in myths. When presented with too many choices, it's helpful to remember that even if someone makes you choose from five hundred ice cream flavors, they're all essentially the same thing: ice cream. The differences are in the details. The same

---

47 Barry Schwartz, *The Paradox of Choice: Why More Is Less* (New York: HarperCollins, 2004), 75.

goes for having too few options. This too is a façade, because is this ever truly the case? There is always a choice, and there is always free will and self-discipline to guide you.

FOOD FOR THOUGHT FROM DR. YOU: The number of choices you have in life depends completely on you. You can decide you have no choice. You can also decide that the world is your oyster. You always have the choice to do something or to do nothing. It is also important to note that, whether patient or caregiver, a health crisis impairs your decision-making for some time. For this reason, do not make rash, important decisions while under the influence of a health crisis: instead, throw the proverbial keys until you are cognizant. Take time to be still, access your power, and regain control when you're ready and able.

HOW TO: You may not always be able to choose your circumstance, but you can always choose how you react to it. You can choose to close your eyes to your options, or you can choose to only focus on one thing. You can choose to allow yourself to be overwhelmed and not move forward because you are hesitant to make a choice, or you can feel like even having two options is two too many. Similarly to the prior time-traveling exercise, the perception of choice is unique to each person. Some people tend to feel trapped with lack of choice. Others may feel overwhelmed with too many choices. Some of that perception depends on how much mental executive function you have left for the day. Either way you choose, it's always important to be objective and honest about your available choices and your role in decision-making. Answer the following questions to see where your choices may take you.

It's a Friday evening, and you have just walked in the door from a long work week. Your phone rings. Do you answer it?

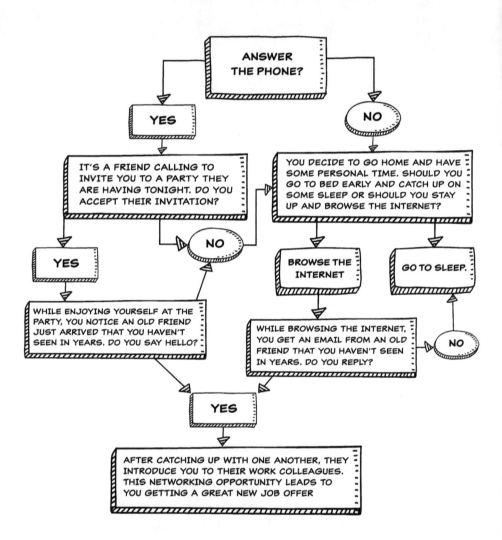

EXCUSE 7: I'LL WAIT FOR A BETTER OPTION.

Working under this myth means you don't change your behaviors now because you believe that a better option or a miracle cure will be available at a later date, perhaps a pill or medical procedure that can cure anything. The truth is that your body is the most complex piece of equipment that you will ever own. Imagine your car breaks down. We all know that it's not always simple to go in and replace one component to get it running again. Oftentimes, one malfunction causes another malfunction, and before you know it, you are stuck with a big bill and a stalled car. You could replace half the car, and it still will not ever work the same way as it did before. Many cars that have been in a car accidents, for example, never run optimally again. If the car is this complicated, imagine the human body.

The body is millions of times more sophisticated, and the hardest truth of all is that not all of its parts are replaceable. Even those that are replaceable are costly and invasive to restore. Like car trouble, your health can break down quickly at the most inopportune times. As many people know, health can change catastrophically overnight. Recovery can be long and complicated and require much time and effort. There are no options available that can deliver the type of turn-around that many of us have somehow convinced ourselves is possible. There is no miracle cure. This is why you must start maintaining your body in the same way you maintain your car. It's not rocket science, but for all the reasons we've discussed so far in this chapter, it's a lot more complicated than it seems.

> **FOOD FOR THOUGHT FROM DR. YOU:** You need to be deliberate about your body's maintenance. There is great value in thinking ahead and being proactive about your healthcare rather than being reactive.

HOW TO: Have you seen any true miracles happen? Some of us can say yes, but for the majority of us, we can't think of one thing. Health is no different. Though there have been "miracle cures" in the past, you decide if there are cures below you'd be willing to try. Match the health issues below with its "miracle cure." [48*]

1: INCONTINENCE	**A. RADIUM WATER**
2: CANCER	**B. GASOLINE**
3: IMPOTENCE	**C. VAGINAL CRYSTAL EGG**
4: LICE	**D. SNAKE VENOM**
5: TEETHING	**E. STARVATION DIET**
6: ANEURYSM	**F. MORPHINE**

In addition to being a fun exercise, this is meant to illustrate how far-fetched some miracle cures can be. As we've mentioned, however, when you're in the throes of a health crisis, you can feel desperate. Instead of putting your hopes in specific cures, put your hope in Dr. You, your team of doctors, your loved ones, and yourself. This creates an optimistic spirit that can be as beneficial as any snake oil.

EXCUSE 8: I LOOK HEALTHY, SO I DON'T NEED TO MAKE CHANGES.

This is a myth I didn't fully understand until I had a young friend diagnosed with cancer. She relayed to me her frustration that people continued to offer their condolences with the tagline, "I don't under-

---

48   48* Answers: 1: C, 2: D, 3: A, 4: B, 5: F, 6: E

stand; I mean, you *look* great." After she pointed this out to me, I started to notice this pattern in others as well. Why do we feel the need to tell people after major illnesses, "Well, you look great!" As if that is some salve that makes them feel like their crisis is less significant or somehow even good for them. I have another friend who is an Instagram influencer who is young, trim, and attractive. Her Instagram feed shows her oceanside yoga poses, her smoothies served with mint leaves in mason jars, her crystals lined up under the full moon. That's the myth. The reality is that she lives hard, drinks hard, smokes hard. But because she looks good and uses the right filter on photos, her health is presumed.

Perhaps this myth is entangled with our culture. There is a lot of pressure by celebrities and social media influencers to cultivate facades of health and wellness. Health decisions are oftentimes driven by external appearance rather than internal well-being. Traditionally this was mostly seen in women and their dogged pursuit of maintained appearances. Because of the rise of social media, we are now seeing this trend in all demographics, regardless of age or gender.

One of my employees experienced this type of judgment in the reverse way. She had severe back issues and therefore had a handi-capped tag on her car. She told me that on a number of occasions she had been confronted by people in parking lots for being "too young and healthy looking" to park in a handicapped space. At one point, in fact, someone even stole the handicapped tag from her car to prove their point.

We have to acknowledge that our world is so much more toxic than it used to be, so this myth will certainly evolve. As our planet continues to become more toxic, the numbers of young people getting ill will unfortunately grow. It used to be that if somebody died in their thirties, it was an overdose, accident, or self-inflicted. Now young people are dying from heart attacks and cancers at alarming rates. According to one study, the annual rate of acute myocardial infarction in young people aged thirty-five to fifty-four-years old rose from 27 percent in 1995–1999 to 32 percent in 2010–1014, with a significant increase in young women.[49] Furthermore, in February 2019, research by the American Cancer Society showed rates of cancer linked to obesity are rising in adults under fifty. Even more alarming is the fact that the younger the generation, the greater the risk of developing certain cancers.[50]

FOOD FOR THOUGHT FROM DR. YOU: Nothing good comes from judging others or even your own health based on appearances. You don't know the nuances of others' health any better than you know the nuances of their thoughts. Similarly, focusing too much on your own external image may be preventing you from looking within to make sure you really are living your optimal life.

HOW TO: It is easy to look at somebody and project our own insecurities, biases, and judgments onto them. The antidote to judgment is empathy, but how do we train ourselves to be empathetic? By starting with ourselves. Using the spaces below, answer the questions as honestly as you can.

49 Alice White, Aaron Folsom, Lloyd Chambless, Richey Sharret, Kiduk Yang, David Conwill, Millicent Higgins, Dale Williams, H. A. Tyroler. "Community surveillance of coronary heart disease in the Atherosclerosis Risk in Communities (ARIC) Study: Methods and initial two years' experience," *Journal of Clinical Epidemiology* 49, no. 2 (February 1996): 223–233. https://www.jclinepi.com/article/0895-4356(95)00041-0/pdf.

50 Rebecca Siegel, Kimberly Miller, and Ahmedin Jemal. "Cancer Statistics 2019," *CA: A Cancer Journal for Clinicians* 69, no. 1 (January 2019): 7–34.

1. **BASED ON YOUR GENDER, WHAT MIGHT PEOPLE ASSUME ABOUT YOU?**

   _____

   _____

2. **BASED ON YOUR RACE, WHAT MIGHT PEOPLE ASSUME ABOUT YOU?**

   _____

   _____

3. **BASED ON YOUR BODY TYPE, WHAT MIGHT PEOPLE ASSUME ABOUT YOU?**

   _____

   _____

4. **BASED ON HOW YOU SPEAK, WHAT MIGHT PEOPLE ASSUME ABOUT YOU?**

   _____

   _____

Look at your responses. Are any of these true? Though some might be accurate, you are likely to feel that the majority would be an unfair or incomplete assessment of you. For us to assume that a person's exterior indicates what their interior is like is always inaccurate. A person's exterior doesn't portend what might be going on inside of them. Rather than spend our time making wild assumptions, wouldn't our time be better spent asking them how they are or just simply letting them know we're here for them? In becoming more aware of the times we do make these assumptions, we are better poised to withhold our judgments in the future.

If we confront the golden excuses we use to resist healthy living, then we are free to embrace the optimal health that is waiting for us. We can spew a tirade of excuses, but as we've discussed in this chapter, those are often unconscious barriers to care and health. They are rooted in fear of change. No matter your go-to excuse—*I don't have time for this*, or *But my life is different than yours*, or *I will, when I'm done with this*—it is inaccurate and hindering your path to wellness.

Such excuses are the wrong escape from conversations about health. I held all of these excuses at some point in my life until my health became dire enough to free myself from their grips. In order to change, you have to realize these golden excuses just aren't true. The idea that happiness and well-being were somewhere in the future and eventually I'd get to them when I had the time, and when I was less busy or when I had more money, or when I had a better night of sleep, was detrimental to my health. Eventually, I realized that life is way too short to live with the idea that I need to be miserable now to be happy later.

Before we even get into the specifics of a Wellness Game Plan in the next chapter, we need to learn to identify and catch ourselves when we make excuses and quickly abandon them. We must realize that though they have been reliable to us over our lives, they're really not good friends of ours, and we just need to let them go. In their absence, there is space for Dr. You to step in and guide you through daily decision-making that can start you—and keep you—on your path to wellness.

EXAM NOTES:

- ☞ Once we feel good, we have a tendency to return to our old routines. We forget why we had the desire to change in the first place.

- ☞ Excuses are barriers to your care and often are rooted in subconscious insecurity.

- ☞ Integrating Dr. You into your current and future care plans allows you to shift from dependence to independence.

- ☞ Love yourself enough to do the things today that will ensure your tomorrow.

- ☞ There is great value in thinking ahead and being proactive about your healthcare rather than being reactive.

CHAPTER 8:

WELLNESS GAME PLAN

There are numerous resources on the market to help you create healthy routines—from nutrition plans and exercise protocols to books, videos, and apps. But, as discussed in our last chapter, sometimes having a plethora of options can be paralyzing. On the flip side, doing nothing is just about the worst thing you can do for your health. So rather than put forth any new health plans for you, I'm going to help distill all of the options into a Wellness Game Plan. From there, you and Dr. You can determine the right plan that will serve as your roadmap to daily wellness and optimal health.

We all know how to be healthy—clean diet, exercise, and quality sleep. Those are the basics we all understand, and exciting new research shows we may even be able to figuratively turn certain genes "on or off" based on our lifestyle and environmental factors. There are some larger, more fundamental changes that we also need to make in order to be healthy individuals, communities, and cultures. The foundational piece to accomplish this is rethinking the role healthcare plays in your life. Ideally, paying attention to your health and choices is not just a thing you do when you're sick. It's what you think about every day. It's a daily investment you make that leads to unquantifiable returns later. The way you achieve this is through Dr. You. In making Dr. You an integral part of your daily life, you change the trajectory of your future. With all of the information available on various healthy lifestyle regimens, let's take some time to distill the information and get back to the basic building blocks of a healthy life. Here are a few things to keep in mind as you prepare your Wellness Game Plan.

FOLLOW DR. YOU'S ADVICE. Lifestyle choices dictate your health risks in intricate ways that science is still trying to unravel. For this reason, Wellness Game Plans need to be custom-tailored solutions for your life. Who is qualified for this job? Dr. You, of course. When Dr. You is at the helm of your care, you can cull through the myriad of resources available to determine the ideal Wellness Game Plan for you. Beware of any cult phenomenon. There is nothing wrong with trying things that are the current rage, but make sure that you have consulted with Dr. You to determine whether they are right for you. Furthermore, when your friends tell you they tried a particular diet or supplement or regimen and had amazing results, Dr. You can be the voice of reason to remind you to manage your expectations and not assume that your body will react in the same way.

In order to live at optimum health, your care needs to address the individual health risks you are exposed to. These health risks are just as diverse as the healthcare solutions themselves. People with high-stress jobs, for example, can have a clean diet and exercise daily and still not be addressing all of their health needs. Maybe they also need to implement daily meditations. On the other hand, a fishing guide who spends each day in the natural world that calms her may not need the benefits of meditation as much as moving the body more or strength training. The moment you try to adopt a one-size-fits-all Wellness Game Plan is the beginning of a frustrating journey that may not be the ideal fit for your lifestyle.

FIND PERSONALIZED SOLUTIONS. In order to achieve your optimal health, you must first acknowledge that your body's systems are complex and sophisticated. One of the basic tenets of good health is to understand everything about you is interconnected. The way you feel emotionally, the way you feel physically, and the way you feel mentally are all related and enmeshed. This is why Dr. You is such an integral part of your Wellness Game Plan. Only Dr. You can understand that the stress of your child's problematic social life, for example, might be what's keeping you up at night, causing cluster headaches, and giving you heartburn. When you appreciate the sophistication and interconnectedness of all systems, it becomes easier to create customized solutions. Maybe the solution for the above example isn't popping headache medicine and antacids; maybe it's talking with your child about their school life and finding some resources that can help them navigate their problem. When we use medicine, diets, and exercise as Band-Aids rather than solutions, we miss the mark on achieving optimal health.

We talked in the last chapter about the myth of the miracle cure. Just as there's no miracle cure, there's also no sudden miracle solution either. Going on a wellness journey means getting different opinions, culling through your own research, analyzing your own role in your compromised health, and being accountable to make changes. Patience is so important because most health issues are not easy to solve. This is why you need to arm yourself with fortitude and forgive yourself if you haven't found your healthy balance just yet. Sometimes wellness is less about sudden, major lifestyle changes; sometimes it's about minor changes that you monitor for a prolonged time to gauge their effects. There is no miracle cure; therefore, the journey to recovery will take time, effort, patience, and discipline.

MANAGE YOUR STRESS. Stress is one of the major factors in diminished health. No matter your size, diet, or activity level, if you are stressed, your body is fighting daily, chronic inflammation. You can have the healthiest regimen in the world, but if you deal with chronic stress, you become like the mythical Sisyphus pushing the *same* boulder up the *same* hill every day. Despite the work you do, you never get closer to your goal.

Much research has been done on the link between stress and disease. We are not talking about the short-term stress of having a flat tire or doing your taxes. Those are events that your body has natural processes to help alleviate. Your body cannot, however, manage long-term, chronic stress. In fact, new research has shown that long-term stress can have systemic effects on the body and compromises almost all of its functions, including the following:

⇨ SUPPRESSES THE IMMUNE SYSTEM

⇨ RAISES THE RISK OF VIRAL INFECTION

⇨ RELEASES HISTAMINE, WHICH CAN TRIGGER ASTHMA

⇨ INCREASES THE RISK FOR DIABETES MELLITUS

⇨ ALTERS THE ACID CONCENTRATION IN THE STOMACH, WHICH CAN LEAD TO PEPTIC ULCERS, STRESS ULCERS, OR ULCERATIVE COLITIS

⇨ LEADS TO PLAQUE BUILDUP IN THE ARTERIES

⇨ CORRELATES WITH PSYCHIATRIC ILLNESS

⇨ SUPPRESSES NATURAL KILLER (NK) CELLS, WHICH ARE INVOLVED IN PREVENTING CANCER[51]

---

51 Mohd. Razali Salleh, "Life Event, Stress and Illness," *The Malaysian Journal of Medical Sciences* 15, no. 4 (October 2008): 9–18. https://www.ncbi.nlm.nih.gov/pmc/articles/PMC3341916/.

Everybody deals with stress, so we all should have strategies to relieve it. The strategies that work for me might not work for you. One person might like walks outside, another might want to spend an hour doing crossword puzzles, someone else might need to sweat their stress out or nap it away. Luckily, with Dr. You as your wellness coach and adviser, you will find the right activities that work for you. When you take a little bit of time every day to take care of your health, you avoid bigger, more complex, more expensive, and ultimately more damaging consequences for your health down the line.

WORK YOUR WAY TO BETTER HEALTH. How you spend eight hours of your day has a lot to do with how happy and healthy you are. The role your job plays in your healthcare is tricky. Sometimes professions are used as excuses. For example, "I work too much to be healthy" or "No matter how healthy I try to be, my stressful job brings me down." Though there is validity in these statements, you cannot use your job as a barrier to good health. As we've discussed in previous chapters, you can be happy and joyful, no matter what your job is, because these emotional states are rooted in choice. You choose happiness; you choose joy. This is an aspect of health that I struggle with daily, and as more people stay in the workforce for longer spans of years, we all need to spend some time addressing how jobs affect health.

Another way jobs can impede our health is that sometimes we can't miss work to seek medical care. This is clearly a problem with the system as a whole, but on a personal level, this conflict can cause catastrophic damage to a person's care and treatment. Healthcare should not be a luxury, but the reality is that it often is. An employee should not have to fret about taking time from work to see about a knee injury, for example. This work/health conflict leads many people to "tough out" their health issues or try to work around them. This often leads to more financial costs and personal damage down the line.

When you have a painful, acute injury that affects your quality of life, you are more likely to go see about treatment than you are for an invisible, mental health issue that doesn't cause external pain or physical dysfunction. Imagine that a person is worried about taking time off work to see about their bad knee. If that is a complicated decision, then imagine the barriers they might face in seeking treatment for a mental health issue. Mental health treatment and care has become a luxury in this country. Mental issues, like ruminating thoughts that keep you awake all night, have the same impact on your quality of life, but because they don't cause pain, bruising, or swelling, we tend to work around them. I often wonder if this is why we have seen spikes in suicide rates in this country: from 1999 through 2017, the suicide rate increased 33 percent from 10.5 to 14.0 per 100,000.[52] This is an alarming trend and points to the need for systemic reform and a reevaluation of access to services.

When someone does seek treatment, whether for physical or mental health, the system often ends up treating the symptoms rather than the cause. For example, high anxiety can cause migraines, but instead of treating the core of the problem, which in some cases may be stress, doctors treat the migraine with pain medications. This isn't contributing to the patient's overall health regimen. This kind of medical "patch up" becomes a cycle that ultimately escalates the problem and does not enhance the health of the patient or the system.

> I AM ASSERTING THAT SMALL ACTIONS TAKEN EACH DAY CAN MAKE YOU A LOT HAPPIER AND HEALTHIER.

---

52   Holly Hedegaard, Sally C. Curtin, and Margaret Warner, "Suicide Mortality in the United States 1999–2017," *National Center for Health Statistics* 330 (November 2018). https://www.cdc.gov/nchs/products/databriefs/db330.

The relationship between work stress and health was a huge motivating factor for me to start my at-home health company. I am not suggesting quitting your job or a complete overhaul of your work life, but I am asserting that small actions taken each day can make you a lot happier and healthier. Instead of going on a smoke break during work, for example, you can go on a walking break and smell the roses. No matter how busy you are, you could start your day with a run or a hike, or something you love to do. You can spend fifteen minutes meditating. As I know from experience, those fifteen minutes will give you an hour of productivity. Because, counterintuitively to our culture, when you are feeling good, physically and emotionally, it almost doesn't matter what the details of your life are. It doesn't matter if you work for the most enlightened start-up and are curing cancer, or you have a job selling cars. You will enjoy that job and those tasks more when you feel happy and healthy. You will also enjoy your interactions with human beings a lot more. You will be more focused and able to effectively perform what you have to do. You will gain the time spent meditating or exercising back and then some because if you are more focused and more productive, then time will fly, and you will do things a lot faster than you typically would. Strangely enough, you get more time by spending more time, as long as the time spent is on quality endeavors and things you love.

As an entrepreneur, I'm often thought of as being the ultimate master of my professional destiny. Although it tickles me to think about, I do acknowledge that there is a lot of truth in this statement because I do tend to march to my own beat and seek out risks. Despite the personal freedoms that sometimes accompany entrepreneurship, there is instability in lifestyle and high personal risks with time, career choices, and financial assets. Seeking risks like these seem to come at an even higher price than many realize.

Psychiatrist Dr. Michael Freeman led a study on the mental health of entrepreneurs and found that 72 percent of those sampled reported mental health concerns, which was significantly higher than the comparison group.[53] As we discussed earlier, our overall health is made up of a multitude of interconnected systems, so if an entrepreneur's mental health is affected, it is a safe assumption that all systems are affected. In other words, the people studied by Dr. Freeman are not people who live in hard conditions; these aren't people who are necessarily drinking, smoking, or doing things that we typically associate with high health risks. Instead these are people who may just work too hard, not sleep enough, and live with hidden anxiety and stress. Maybe they worry endlessly about being responsible for the well-being, not just of themselves, but of their families and of the people they employ.

I recently spoke as a guest lecturer for graduate business students at the University of Southern California. The goal was to serve as entrepreneur-in-residence to talk to the students about entrepreneurial challenges and offer advice to prepare them for life after school. The professor asked that I talk about how to land your first one hundred clients. I thought, *No problem.* As I prepared my lectures, however, I realized that I can give advice on how to get customers, but that's not all there is to it. I thought back to the early days of my career performing cold calls and placating rude customers. I realized it was jobs I hated the most that taught me how to persevere, how to not take *no* for an answer, how on the worst and busiest days, there's always time for self-care because if there wasn't, I would have given up—even worse, I would have fallen apart. I decided to restructure my talk, and ended up focusing on the key to success as an entrepreneur—making time and room to learn and take care of yourself.

---

53 Michael Freeman, "Are Entrepreneurs 'Touched with Fire?'" last modified April 17, 2015, http://www.michaelafreemanmd.com/Research_files/ Are%20Entrepreneurs%20Touched%20with%20Fire%20(pre-pub%20 n)%204-17-15.pdf.

I figured these students had gotten earfuls of business tactics, but did they really know how to survive in this cutthroat world? Did they know that they had to make time for themselves and their well-being? It's the one tactic I most certainly never heard anyone mention in my business school days and the one that has been most valuable to me in my career. After my talk, I was surprised by the students' reactions. Many came up to me after the lecture and said, "We've never heard anybody else talk about this. They always tell us about networking skills, interview tips, and how to create budgets. Nobody has talked to us about self-care." Though my talk was somewhat of a no-brainer, their response was rooted in the traditional business training, where soft skills are rarely discussed. I hope that by putting health into the context of business, I might get through to them, and it seemed I had. After all, if you learn discipline and perseverance in your fitness and athletic realms, you can apply those same skills to the business world. If more upcoming entrepreneurs are proactive about their health and well-being, perhaps the statistics will change about the personal risks of entrepreneurship.

For business owners, health insurance is expensive. Whether you buy it for yourself or provide it for others, it is a huge expense. Oftentimes as an entrepreneur, you may figure you don't need that expense. *I'm healthy now*, you may think, *so do I really need it?* This goes back to the myth of invincibility, and many self-employed people fall prey to it. If a health issue does arise—and the statistics suggest it will—it becomes challenging to take care of your health. When you're an entrepreneur, you don't have the luxury of sick leave, vacation time, and paid leave. So every hour, every day, that you take off from your business ultimately has a much bigger financial cost than just the rendering of the services because you may lose revenue, or you may even lose a deal or a contract. This is the reason entrepreneurs, especially in the earlier stages of their businesses, avoid buying health insurance or seeking medical care when they need it. Unfortunately this makes seeking preventative care much more challenging, and we can see from the above statistics how detrimental this potentially is.

The other thing that entrepreneurs oftentimes suffer from is a sense of isolation because they don't have/find the time to connect to people around them. Sometimes they don't think people around them will understand them, and perhaps they're right, but nonetheless, finding like-minded people and support networks is vital to their health.

If you are an entrepreneur, you need Dr. You by your side to reaffirm what your intuition might be telling you about your health. Dr. You needs to nudge you to take the stairs rather than the elevator or needs to guide you on regular meditations that might help you relieve the pressure of a field that is proven to be high risk. Entrepreneurs are a rare breed of visionary risk takers. Let Dr. You remind you, however, that no reward is worth the risk of compromised health.

BE PROACTIVE. Rather than provide you with the generic health tips we all know, like exercise two to three times a week, eat healthy, get some sleep, I'd rather remind you of the areas of your life to cultivate. The healthiest individuals I know are also master balancers. They know the areas in life to spend their energy and time on, and they find the balance that works for them. Use the categories below to take an inventory of how much time and attention you give to each area weekly. Decide what you could actively do today to honor each category in your life. Find the balance that works for you.

PHYSICAL HEALTH: DIET. You don't have to spend all your money on organic berries and wheatgrass shots. Be sensible about your diet and your portions. Maybe you need a high protein diet, maybe you need a vegetarian diet, but only you and Dr. You can decide for sure.

You can also do a lot by doing less when it comes to nutrition. For example, cut back on sugar, alcohol, or caffeine—now that will save you a buck! Find what works for you, and maintain healthy choices that contribute to your optimal health.

PHYSICAL HEALTH: EXERCISE. Don't make this one too complicated; just move your body as often as you can. It doesn't need to be a yoga routine taught by shamans. Just take your dog for a walk, take the stairs, or park your car in the far corner of the parking lot.

MENTAL HEALTH. Find things that quiet your mind and make you happy. Maybe it's a walk in nature, maybe it's knitting, maybe it's listening to Enya. Find what works for you, and do it often. Exercise your brain like you do your body—solve puzzles, learn a new language, and keep a positive level of intellectual challenge in your life. Another factor worth mentioning is the growing awareness that our microbiome—the balance of microorganisms and bacteria in our gut—plays a crucial role in our mental and emotional health. Always look at the big picture.

SOCIAL HEALTH. Connect to people, talk to friends, build a network of support. If you don't have family, it's OK, because families can be built from the support systems around us. Surround yourself with people who are concerned about your well-being, and work hard to cultivate and maintain these connections.

EMOTIONAL HEALTH. Choose happiness and joy. Ask for help when you need it. Allow yourself to be vulnerable. Allow yourself to cry, grieve, and even be angry on occasion. Bottled-up emotions can create long-lasting trauma impacting your subconscious. Treat yourself well.

By creating a Wellness Game Plan for yourself using the categories above, you are becoming your own hero, your own advocate, your own Dr. You. You are demanding a higher quality of life and wellness. In changing this for yourself and your family, we can begin to shift a paradigm that has been failing us for generations. Take a moment to make some objective observations about your own balance in the above categories. Think of personalized ways you can begin to find balance in these areas of your life, starting today.

PHYSICAL HEALTH: DIET

HOW MUCH TIME I CURRENTLY SPEND ON THIS WEEKLY:

_____

HOW MUCH TIME I WOULD LIKE TO SPEND ON THIS WEEKLY:

_____

GOALS/CHANGES/ROUTINES I COULD START THIS WEEK TO CULTIVATE THIS AREA OF MY LIFE:

_____

_____

PHYSICAL HEALTH: EXERCISE

HOW MUCH TIME I CURRENTLY SPEND ON THIS WEEKLY:

_____

HOW MUCH TIME I WOULD LIKE TO SPEND ON THIS WEEKLY:

_____

ACTIVITIES I COULD START THIS WEEK TO CULTIVATE THIS AREA OF MY LIFE:

_____

_____

MENTAL HEALTH

HOW MUCH TIME I CURRENTLY SPEND ON THIS WEEKLY:

_____

HOW MUCH TIME I WOULD LIKE TO SPEND ON THIS WEEKLY:

_____

ACTIVITIES/GOALS/CHANGES/ROUTINES I COULD START THIS WEEK TO CULTIVATE THIS AREA OF MY LIFE:

_____

_____

SOCIAL HEALTH

HOW MUCH TIME I CURRENTLY SPEND ON THIS WEEKLY:

_____

HOW MUCH TIME I WOULD LIKE TO SPEND ON THIS WEEKLY:

_____

ACTIVITIES/GOALS/CHANGES/ROUTINES I COULD START THIS
WEEK TO CULTIVATE THIS AREA OF MY LIFE:

_____

_____

EMOTIONAL HEALTH

HOW MUCH TIME I CURRENTLY SPEND ON THIS WEEKLY:

_____

HOW MUCH TIME I WOULD LIKE TO SPEND ON THIS WEEKLY:

_____

ACTIVITIES/GOALS/CHANGES/ROUTINES I COULD START THIS
WEEK TO CULTIVATE THIS AREA OF MY LIFE:

_____

_____

When it comes to integrating Dr. You into your Wellness Game
Plan, I am often reminded of the Thai Health Promotion Foundation's
antismoking campaign. Understanding the power of self-awakening,
they created a message that was meant for and ultimately given by
the smoker themselves: "To create a real behavior change, we had to
select the right speaker, one who smokers will trust wholeheartedly.
And there is no more powerful envoy of the anti-smoking message
than the smokers themselves."[54] The video, called "Smoking Kid,"

---

54   "Smoking Kid," Thai Health Promotion Foundation, https://aef.com/wp-
     content/uploads/2017/02/award-2013chiat-thpf-smoking-kid-case.pdf.

shows a montage of adults smoking absentmindedly when a young child comes up to them holding a cigarette and asks, "Can I get a light?" The adults pause for a moment, considering the absurdity of the situation before responding.

SMOKER 1:

"I'm not giving it to you."

SMOKER 2:

"Smoking is bad; you have to stop."

SMOKER 3:

"Cigarettes contain insecticides."

SMOKER 4:

"You look old when you smoke."

SMOKER 5:

"If you smoke, you die faster. Don't you want to live and play?"

SMOKER 6:

"You know it's bad, right? When you smoke, you suffer from lung cancer, emphysema, and strokes."

The child then asks, "So why are you smoking?" The child then hands the smoker a pamphlet that reads, "You worry about me. But why not about yourself? Reminding yourself is the most effective warning to help you quit. Call 1600 hotline to quit smoking." After this video aired, the hotline calls increased 40 percent; and in five days, the video was viewed five million times.[55] What was so successful about this campaign was that the creators understood that the most powerful speaker we listen to is ourselves.

---

55   "Smoking Kid," YouTube video, 2:37, posted by "Ogilvy," June 6, 2013, https://www.youtube.com/watch?v=g_YZ_PtMkw0.

For this reason, Dr. You is sometimes the only one we will listen to. We all know that hearing an external voice telling us to change our behavior rarely results in action. When we have a recognition, an epiphany, that the desire for change originates in us, then we can make some monumental behavioral and lifestyle changes. Like the anti-smoking campaign, Dr. You can be a good reminder to treat ourselves the way we want to treat a child.

WELLNESS IS LESS ABOUT DIET AND EXERCISE AND MORE ABOUT A SHIFT IN THINKING.

Creating a Wellness Game Plan and reviewing it daily creates a paradigm shift that will benefit us for generations. Wellness is less about diet and exercise and more about a shift in thinking. A fundamental part of the culture is seeking healthcare when we're sick. Instead, we need to think about health daily. You don't feed your dog only when it's howling and starving; you feed it daily so it won't get to that point. You must start thinking of your health in the same way.

In order to devise and maintain our Wellness Game Plan, we need to get to know ourselves better, and we need to understand and enjoy that relationship. We spend a lot of time and attention getting to know our intimate partners or our friends, but how about we divert some of that energy toward getting to know ourselves, our bodies, our needs? What activities and routines make us the best versions of ourselves? Are we eating our best diet? Are we following our best exercise regimen? Or are we doing things that inadvertently prevent us from performing at our optimum? We must remember there is an ongoing, proactive lifestyle we can embrace that increases our access to optimal health—our Wellness Game Plan.

As you are establishing your Wellness Game Plan, make sure you continue to cultivate patience, empathy, and self-love. It's not just for others; it's for yourself. Once you have established these qualities in relation to yourself, you can then offer them to others. As you continue on this journey, there will be a lot of things to figure out and a lot of time spent searching, so continue to return to these hallmarks of wellness: patience, empathy, love.

On your wellness journey, be your best friend. Show up for yourself in the same way you would show up for others. Give yourself patience, love, and kindness in this process. Without integrating self-love, then diet plans and exercise regimens can be used to beat ourselves down. You are not creating your Wellness Game Plan to "fix" things that are "wrong" with you. It's not a certain body you are trying to attain, or a certain inflammation level you're seeking; it's self-love you are after. Let Dr. You step in when you are being unkind to yourself or pushing yourself too hard. Just as a doctor is compassionate and empathetic toward patients, let Dr. You be a daily model of how to be that for yourself. Use these pages to find balance in your life and to devise a Wellness Game Plan that allows you to love yourself and the life you've built at every step of your journey.

EXAM NOTES:

- Find personalized solutions, and follow Dr. You's advice.

- Manage your stress.

- Work your way to better health.

- Be proactive.

- Find your balance between physical health, mental health, emotional health, and social health.

9

CHAPTER 9:

WHAT'S AHEAD

was recently talking with a friend who was sharing his frustrations about the time it takes to deal with the multiple suppliers in his industry. He said there was no easy way to get bids or quotes because there was no centralized system where you can enter parameters and get a comparison of estimates across the board. As he was talking, my entrepreneurial "spidey sense" kicked in, and I suddenly got excited. I declared, "That's great! There isn't anything available on the market, and if people are as frustrated as you are, they would pay a lot of money to have access to software that solves the problem." He snapped, "No, you're not listening to me! I'm the expert in this field, and you're telling me something can be done when I know it can't be. If it could be done, somebody would have already done it." I was confounded. I told him I was listening, and that is precisely why and how I recognized an opportunity, because everything I've ever built in my life has come after I was told it can't be done or someone else would have already done it.

My company, myLAB Box, is a perfect example of this. My cofounder and I spent two years being asked, "Why you? Who are you to do this?" and being told, "No, it's not possible." What I realized was that some people take *no* for an answer, and some people don't. Those of us with the entrepreneurial mindset go against the status quo and seek challenges that we're confident we can solve. In fact, the challenges actually fuel us, not discourage us. What was interesting about my conversation with my friend was that the same situation can lead to innovation in one individual and frustration in another. Although I wasn't able to convince my friend to take on the challenge, I did leave the conversation thinking about what it takes to enact change. I decided it's some unique alchemy of personality and circumstance.

There are people who have health issues every single day, who get frustrated with their care or barriers, who feel desperate, and who inevitably suffer through their frustrations with varying rates of success. What was different for me on my health journey was that I did not want to accept that there were no better alternatives. I refused to believe the process was as good as it could be. I don't expect all to share my entrepreneurial mindset, but I do hope that this book energizes you enough not to settle for the status quo in your healthcare. Frustration and desperation are inevitable, but your journey does not have to end there.

My personal story has continued to evolve even in recent years. After starting my company in 2013, I lived pedal-to-the-metal, no days off, working until the wee hours every day. After four years of this, I experienced a significant decline in my health, and, once again, I was unable to receive any answers from doctors. I spent thousands on lab tests and consultations with different experts, who, after eight months, were nowhere closer to telling me what the issue was. Though reaching another dead end with my health was frustrating, it also inspired me to keep challenging myself and my own innovation. What could I do to change the system?

MYLAB BOX: WHAT'S NEXT

With myLAB Box, we initially focused on the diagnostic space because we wanted to address the spread of disease, but as we were evolving and learning more about what optimal health means, the preventative part of healthcare seemed to garner more importance for us. My hope is that the myLAB Box tests will provide insights unlike anything else we have had in the past, and as the science evolves, these tests will deliver even more beneficial results.

One area we find extremely important in our company, beyond testing and getting insights, is how we turn information into action. Would knowing you might be predisposed to certain ailments mean that you immediately need to change your diet? Would you instantly make radical changes in your livelihood? Most likely not, but it does mean that you would monitor certain conditions more closely. Maybe it means you consider implementing incremental changes and consulting with experts to decide the best course of action for reaching optimum health. We are excited to see how our evolving system ends up connecting with people. Being able to develop the first testing-to-treatment platform nationwide into a system that connects you not only to physicians, but also connects you to health coaches and dieticians, and gives you immediate access to the tools that you need to take steps based on your health data, is key to unlocking major innovations.

Unfortunately, due to the way our healthcare system has been constructed in the United States all of these systems have been separated. You go into a generalist to be tested; then the generalist refers you to a specialist; then the specialist does more testing and refers you elsewhere. During that journey, people oftentimes get discouraged, disillusioned, and lost. Information also gets lost. The process is convoluted, complicated, and void of continuity of care. This is why it is imperative that myLAB Box and others innovations like it offer a hub that allows this journey to become transparently integrated.

In the book *Connected*, by Nicholas Christakis, he considers how things spread—from viruses to behavior and social patterns. He discusses how our social networks and the way that we are interconnected ultimately determines how things travel between us. Using viruses as a model of how adaptive and connected something can be, we realize that the medical community has major chasms. Viruses are beating the academics and the clinicians, because they are responding instantly and immediately to the changing landscape, and benefiting from the increase in connections inadvertently. The only way to curb a disease is to be able to diagnose and treat it faster than it can spread. Unless we tactically adapt a radical new way of diagnosing and treating disease, viruses will continue to win. In this same way, unless we devise better systems of communication and adaptation, we will not curb the spread of ineffective healthcare processes.

As a pioneer of the healthcare industry, I considered how the themes of *Connected* apply to diagnostics. How can we ultimately leverage social connection and a new paradigm of interconnectivity to curb the spread of disease and change behavior in a positive fashion? We need to make a conscious effort to leverage connections for diagnostic purposes, and this is particularly what myLAB Box has endeavored to do, unlike any of its predecessors. To date, the biggest driver for the company has been social connection. This starts through word of mouth reaching people, one at a time, and allowing information to go viral (pun intended). Ultimately, these connections can be as viral as viruses themselves. This is what's really exciting about the way we are approaching this differently than the incumbents in the space.

Viruses seek to connect with receptors in a host. Humans work a bit like that as well, except they have biases and opinions that oftentimes get in the way of those connection. As we've seen in the political realm, presenting facts to somebody who already has formed an opinion doesn't tend to actually dissuade them from that opinion; in fact, it tends to ingrain them in that opinion. These emotional biases can unfortunately blind us to the truth. Despite our human fallacies, however, the opportunity is there, and we are positioned in a unique way to have these realizations as a global community and start living with a new level of awareness. This evolution will require a certain momentum and a public that has adapted their thought processes to the way that information disseminates today. There's a lot of criticism around how young generations are absorbed with social media, but it gives me hope because the way that this new generation is intercon-nected is something unprecedented.

In a 1983 paper by anthropologist and evolutionary psycholo-gist Robin Dunbar, he studied the correlation between brain size and group size in primates and concluded that humans, based on our brain size, should have social groups of about 150 people.[56] The whole idea that we're only capable of connecting with 150 people will certainly be challenged because there's a new metric now that we need to look at. Maybe we are only connected to a certain number, but how many others are we able to influence?

There is a growing number of people who aspire to being social media influencers. We don't know what will come of these more distant human connections, but they might hold the potential to effect more change than face-to-face connections. I can speculate on all the ways these developing connections will change the industry, but no matter the specifics of the changes, there will no doubt be a thought evolution

---

56   R. Dunbar, "Coevolution of Neocortex Size, Group Size, and Language in Humans," *Behavioral and Brain Sciences* 16 (1993): 681–735.

that takes place in the way that we filter information. We haven't seen this growing generation enter the healthcare sphere quite yet, but we have seen their impact on other areas. The recent movements around gun control, for example, gave us a glimpse of the power this new generation has to mobilize and organize on issues that affect them. Anyone who pays attention will notice a true potential revolution in the way this new generation operates.

When I look at systems that are so deeply ingrained in terms of behaviors, like the medical community, the most likely driver of change will not come from the inside, through evolution; it will come from the outside, in the form of revolution. I think myLAB Box has been an example of disruption so powerful that it sends a message with ripple effects through the business space, the healthcare space, and maybe eventually even the political space. Just a few short years after our launch, we see the biggest lab networks also now seeking ways to make testing available on the go, with more and more alternatives becoming available every day. I hope that as my company grows, this message will continue reaching people. We have already disrupted the laboratory testing space, and we started an incredible wave of direct-to-consumer solutions. In order for us to continue this type of disruption, we need to garner the momentum through massive volumes of people.

I see similar advancements happening in commerce through start-ups like myLAB Box or one of the more vertically integrated companies making solid claims in the healthcare space. As people connect and influence change and the commerce world does the same, the medical community and the political space will catch up. If they don't, then they're not paying attention, and we have a much bigger problem. This is the paradigm of the future, and if medical institutions fail to adapt, fail to improve, or fail to acknowledge the end user's need for a positive user experience, they'll lose traction, as many have already. I wish I had more hope in the abilities of the systems to see the signs and adapt, but the truth is, I don't see it happening, and that is partly because there's a lot of incentive in the insurance, payer, and the political spaces to keep the status quo.

Given the resources and burgeoning connectedness our society has, it's clear what we need to do and the direction we need to take: we need to leverage our resources and embrace the changes that are happening and move with them, just like a virus. This is our challenge to creators, doers, business owners, and institutions. Beyond a diagnosis for disease, this has the potential to optimize well-being and create pathways and channels for wellness to propagate throughout communities and peer groups, locally and globally.

In the same way that disease spreads and diagnostics can travel, so does awareness, and we sometimes underestimate the power of individual action in this picture. By taking better care of my health, I inadvertently affect several degrees of individuals around me, whether I'm aware of it or not. Sharing positive health journeys online and talking about our experiences, from depression to allergies, creates opportunities for dialogue. These conversations make space for awareness, and we are then more open to the possibility of finding solutions sooner rather than later. Engaging in conversations about solutions means that the paths to success can now be shared with more than an individual. When we struggle in silence, we help no one. My company, myLAB Box, only scratches the surface of the diagnostic options that we could make available—and should make available—so that when health issues arise, we have an affordable and easy way to identify problems. Let's consider some of the other innovations that are fueling positive trends that could change the way we think of and interact with the healthcare system.

INNOVATIONS IN HEALTHCARE

Most of the brainpower in the healthcare field has traditionally been focused on devices and pharmaceuticals. Perhaps the greatest reason for this is that it's exciting to work on these scientific challenges. Unfortunately, the more common reason is because this is a lucrative field of study. If you are the first one to start printing organs for transplants, for example, it comes with a monumental payoff. Things that you can patent and control access to secure your investment. For this reason, devices and pharmaceuticals have historically drawn much brain power and capital, which has unfortunately resulted in some less lucrative advancements being overlooked. Another drawback of putting all our resources into these areas is that these innovations may not impact our current generation. Even though many technologies have been created, they require validation through the FDA approval process. This can take years before an average consumer can gain access to them.

Other areas that historically don't garner as much attention and capital are less obvious, like how we interface with laboratories and the way that we get our results. We are seeing advancements in the self-collection space, which again shows the trend toward making access to lab results more instantaneous and accessible without the invasive procedures of the past. In a day-to-day scenario, a lot more people are dealing with challenges around scheduling doctor visits, taking time off work to see a specialist, getting their lab work done, and having access to care, rather than needing organ printing. While these more subtle innovations may be less profitable per unit of sale, they have greater potential to change more lives. The fact that there are now more companies coming into the consumer health space that are looking at these less obvious innovations is a positive trend that has the potential to transform healthcare.

WEARABLE DEVICES. One of the biggest shifts in recent years is the trend of wearables entering the marketplace. As primitive as they still are in both their science and their execution, they've created an appetite in the consumer for personalized solutions. With this has come an interest in gaining immediate, direct access to individuals' information, results, and outcomes. Though there are certain concerns about how personalized healthcare can get, the trend is moving in the right direction toward personalization of care. Furthermore, it has yet to be seen to what degree personalization can actually result in better outcomes, but it is a promising trend nonetheless.

Even if the trend in personalization utilizes the same treatment, it still ultimately has a different patient care approach from the traditional one—which I consider a success. Conventionally we have had an authoritarian healthcare system where the provider is sovereign and undisputed. It's created a hierarchy in the relationship between physicians, nurses, and patients. Even though it may have been necessary at some point for the functioning of these organizations, it has contributed to the establishment of an impersonal healthcare system where people feel lost and aimless. They need a guide, a mentor, to offer direction. As we discussed in chapter 4, we know those aspects of care can make a huge difference in outcomes. A systemic review of randomized trials reported that:

> Effective communication exerts a positive influence not only on the emotional health of the patient but also on symptom resolution, functional and physiologic status and pain control ... Patients need to feel that they are active participants in care and that their problem has been discussed fully. Patients should share in decision making

when a plan for management is formulated … Agreement between patient and physician about the nature of the problem and the course of action appears to bode well for a successful outcome.[57]

Being a patient who interacts with a compassionate healthcare professional who really is invested in their well-being will improve their chance for and length of recovery. As we've discussed throughout the book, anytime you can find solutions that fit your health and emotional needs, you are on the right path. If innovations in the system can offer patients access to personal information and a mentor figure to guide them through it, then we are fundamentally changing the system.

One direction these wearable devices will ultimately take us is toward a more proactive stance that uses data for preventable care. For example, wearable monitors might show early detection for heart attacks or for certain conditions like diabetes. As we develop new ways to capture this individualized data, we will see more companies using it for preventative care. Apple and Google already aggregate cardio data from users. Ultimately we could potentially save lives if these devices detect an unusual cardiac pattern, for example, and could call 911 for you if you experience a health issue.

There is also a shift happening in how a patient accesses care. First we had wearables on the market; then we saw the rise of smart home devices. The natural next step is the delivery of healthcare services

---

57   Ariëtte R. J. Sanders, Inge van Weeghel, Maartje Vogelaar, William Verheul, Ron H. M. Pieters, Niek J. de Wit, Jozien M. Bensing. "Effects of improved patient participation in primary care on health-related outcomes: a systematic review," *Oxford Journal: Family Practice* 30, no. 4 (April 2013): 1429. https://www.ncbi.nlm.nih.gov/pmc/articles/PMC3722509/#CIT0015.

to the home. We're already starting to do this via e-commerce, but imagine when this gets integrated into Google or Alexa. It's a game changer to have the ability to say, "Hey Google, schedule my dentist appointment" or "Alexa, find an ENT near me." Or even better, if the AI assistant could say, without even being prompted, "I've noticed an elevated blood pressure and irregular heart rate. Would you like me to schedule a call with your primary care physician?" Oscar Health was the first app to introduce the call-a-doctor-on-demand-for-free feature. This is still a primitive system, but eventually we should be able to access specialists on the go ourselves. When the technology gets adopted by more people, we'll see a change in how we interact with doctors and nurses. Perhaps this will lead to better follow-up care and eventually even virtual exams.

MERGING AND EXPANSION OF DISCIPLINES. There is a trend toward the merging of medical disciplines that will make doctors nervous, but will ultimately benefit the patient. Patient-doctor inter-actions will evolve as a result of doctors looking at multiple systems. Your general doctor, your internist, your cardiologist, and any medical professional will likely have to comprehend a much deeper and broader knowledge than they have previously had to in the past.

I recently had the flu, and when I saw my doctor, I told her it felt like something was stuck in my throat. I asked, "Can you look and see if you see anything?" Her response was, "You'll need to go to an ear, nose, and throat specialist for that." Guess what? Months have passed, and I still have yet to schedule that appointment. Why? Because I already spent the time to go the first appointment and didn't get any information. Now I have to spend more time and more money to find a ENT specialist. The medical community needs to recognize that handing off the individual to another doctor just isn't working. Much like any other consumer journey, the more "clicks" you have to make toward a purchase, the less likely you are to complete that purchase. This is a nominal effort interface.

The industry has fragmented itself to the point where it doesn't even make any sense. Why does a *specialist* need to look at my throat? Shouldn't my primary doctor have these basic tools at her disposal to meet my individual needs? Imagine a cosmologist trying to figure out how the universe works by just looking at our solar system and trying to figure out why it is structured the way it is without having any kind of larger understanding of what other solar systems exist. You can't look at things that simplistically. Physicians and health experts must embrace that body, mind, and all systems of the body work together. We can no longer look at them as separate entities just because it's easier on the doctor to specialize. This is not offering quality service to the patient.

PHYSICIANS AND HEALTH EXPERTS MUST EMBRACE THAT BODY, MIND, AND ALL SYSTEMS OF THE BODY WORK TOGETHER.

PERSONALIZED MEDICATIONS. There is also some exciting innovation and research happening in the prescription world. One such example is the ability to create prescriptions and medications that precisely target people and can address viruses or bacteria based on their genetic profiles and physiology. This can save a lot of human suffering by expediting and improving diagnostic processes, not to mention addressing the huge problem of antibiotic overuse. These advancements would allow us to give medications that can target the specific conditions and minimize the impacts on other systems. This is a major component in the trend toward personalized healthcare solutions. The unfortunate thing about pharmaceuticals is that they take a long time to develop and approve. We are now seeing medications available on the market that began their journey twenty years ago. Things that are in the pipeline now based on our current awareness and research may not hit the market until decades from now, which goes back to the need to create a more efficient approval system so we can impact lives today and not decades into the future.

ALTERNATIVE THERAPIES. Another trend in healthcare is the legalization of cannabis products beyond medical use therapies. More markets are opening to them, and this will pave the way for psychedelics, since both have been shown to help with anxiety, depression, and PTSD. This matters because it points to the larger trend we just discussed toward an integrative medicine approach. For decades now, medicine has evolved into a fragmented system of narrow specializations. Physicians, healthcare professionals, and individuals are starting to recognize that although specialized expertise is important, it has resulted in a lack of visibility of the bigger picture and a lack of success in treatment because physicians may be looking at things so narrowly through the prism of their specialty.

VIRTUAL REALITY. A trend that portends the future of healthcare is the use of virtual reality. It is currently being used with great success for patients with phantom limb pain to help patch the ensuing cognitive dissonance. It is also being used to train doctors, especially surgeons, since they can view and manipulate 3-D models of organs. What is most exciting about the virtual reality industry is the potential it holds to create interactive environments that further facilitate self-care.

TISSUE REPAIR. There are also some interesting things in the realm of tissue repair. Typically the military tends to get some innovations first, but we are moving toward having military technology available to the public for treatment. Even though this innovation is about tissue repair, the trend driving it will have huge impacts on treatment and potentially affect surgical interventions and even aesthetic services. Clinical needs often portend aesthetic preference because there's a lot of money in the beauty industry. It would not be surprising if the advancements in body repair don't extend to personalized beauty and aesthetics.

HEALTHCARE SOLUTIONS. The international market has become a more appealing ground for the deployment and utilization of innovative healthcare solutions than the United States. Many Americans are shocked to learn that developing nations gain access to vital treatment solutions ahead of the American public. Australia and Northern European countries, for example, outrank North America in providing care for HIV and achieving viral suppression.[58] Some treatments that are available in international markets are unavailable in the United States due to the regulatory landscape, with its complications and costliness. Because of these challenges, we are depriving ourselves unnecessarily from access to solutions that can change lives. We have the capacity to change these regulatory barriers by joining with businesses, organizations, and healthcare professionals, and demanding they engage in open conversations about our society's needs.

How can we prepare to meet exciting opportunities of tomorrow so we don't miss them right here in the United States? The fact that American companies look to international markets is unfortunate. How can we shift our way of thinking so we can allow for this innovation to gain traction? And how can we rethink our philosophies

---

58　Keith Alcorn, "Australia performs best in HIV treatment cascade– 62% with undetectable viral load," *NAMaidsmap*, November 4, 2014, http://www.aidsmap.com/Australia-performs-best-in-HIV-treatment-cascade-62-with-undetectable-viral-load/page/2919074/.

around risk and around what we're trying to solve with these approvals and processes? Rather than having standardized pricing, which puts it out of reach for some of the most innovative start-ups, what if we could prioritize approvals and determine their cost based on how vital a solution is? Then the Food & Drug Administration, like the United Nations, could set objectives decades ahead to incentivize solving certain health challenges. This would reward start-ups and organizations that are taking risks by allowing them to have a friendlier, more cost effective, and ultimately faster experience in the regulatory process. This would keep them from getting shut down because they run out of capital.

When we were developing myLAB Box, we had to consider national versus international markets. We had access to products that were CE and ISO approved (independent, international, nongovernment standard approvals), and it would have still taken us over $10 million to clear a whole panel for sexual health. It's close to impossible for a company of our size to deliver such products to the US market. That barrier led to many conversations within myLAB Box about whether we should become an international business or not. Ultimately, we chose not to (at least, not at the get-go) because we believe in solving the issues that we see in our local community, in our own country. It wasn't an easy decision to make, and I question it almost daily. It goes back to the entrepreneur mentality. Do you want to create a successful business? Or do you want your creation to be a bridge to a better, more evolved world? We chose the latter.

Unless we see a radical shift in the way that we operate in the United States, the hub of medical innovations will land in a different country. That process has already begun. We might be surprised where it lands, but it will not be America. In the future, we might see much higher involvement from the business end driving solutions to the healthcare sector. I suspect that many big players like Amazon, Google, Walmart, and many others will inevitably make plays in this space in what will ultimately become a deeper and broader consumerization of healthcare. We will see this in the start-up world, and I hope this motivates entrepreneurs who are solving healthcare challenges in new and original ways. Once larger companies bring their capital and influence into the healthcare space, the government and legislative bodies will start paying attention. I am excited for the day the conversation shifts from whether or not we should have insurance and how much we should cover under that insurance to really bigger and broader conversations around diagnostics, preventative care, the optimization of well-being, and the use of these as measures of the quality of life in America and beyond. As a global community, we need to commit to good health being a human right and focus our collective energies around well-being.

The recent drive toward self-discovery seen in innovations around personalized solutions is setting the stage for a host of revolutionary services and devices that could create the human race of the future, one that lives in optimum health for longer spans of life. With innovative advancements like myLAB Box, we are garnering the tools we need to become a healthier population. We have a lot of information and resources, and now is the time to combine those with our societal mechanisms in a way that changes the culture of personalized and self-directed healthcare. When individuals are empowered and informed, we maximize human potential. We can become a generation of people who are armed with facts and no longer have an insurmountable chasm between ourselves and the outdated health practitioners of the past.

EXAM NOTES:

☞ We must devise better systems of communication and adaptation to curb the spread of ineffective healthcare processes.

☞ If medical institutions fail to adapt, fail to improve, or fail to acknowledge the end user's need for a positive user experience, they'll lose traction.

☞ Advocacy has the potential to optimize well-being and create pathways and channels for wellness to propagate throughout communities and peer groups, locally and globally.

☞ Being a patient who interacts with a compassionate healthcare professional who really is invested in their well-being will improve their chance for and length of recovery.

☞ Physicians and health experts must embrace that body, mind, and all systems of the body work together.

CONCLUSION:

IT STARTS WITH YOU AND DR. YOU

For my entire life, my grandmother wished me good health on every holiday. Every birthday, good health. Every Christmas, good health. It drove me crazy because I just wanted to be happy, but she kept wishing me good health instead. I thought that happiness was the ideal state in life. As I got older and battled a series of health issues, I realized she had been right all along: you can't be happy if your health interferes with finding the beauty of this world. As children we're taught to bathe our bodies, clean our teeth, take our vitamins. As youth, we're taught to work diligently and try hard. But where are the lessons that prepare you for how to work hard *and* enjoy life? How can we take care of our bodies, work hard, and enjoy living?

The irony about health is that you need it to enjoy every aspect of life. You can be successful in your career, even if your love life is nonexistent. You can be happy in love, even if your career life is lacking. But you can't enjoy either of these things if your health deteriorates. Can you have a healthy relationship if you are in survival mode all the time? Can you give your work the energy and focus it deserves if all you can think about is the moment you can lie in bed and make the pain cease by falling asleep?

Considering that US healthcare spending grew 3.9 percent in 2017, reaching $3.5 trillion, which accounts for 17.9 percent of the nation's gross domestic product, why is the current healthcare system actually losing people?[59] What happens when people are paying cash for their care, for example, and why are they doing this? How does this impact their outcomes and engagement? This shows not only how bad the system has gotten, but also what people are willing to do to compensate for a broken system. The current healthcare system gives the American people two options: play with the system and potentially suffer, or pay a lot more out of pocket to get better outcomes.

Making decisions without advocating for yourself—without having Dr. You—ends up in many cases costing money and quality of life. To be a health advocate, you need to ask questions and be informed about your options. Advocacy is like having a retirement account. Imagine being able to withdraw from that account every single day of your life, knowing that it can't be depleted. In fact, the more you withdraw, the more your dividends grow, the better you get at protecting your healthcare interests, the more you can withdraw every day, and the more you'll end up with in the end. You're investing in a better quality life, a longer life, fewer health complications, less damage to your body, faster recovery times, and better care for your loved ones. Let this book be a resource to take control of your health so that you don't have to spend thousands on it later.

When things in life get bad enough—whether in relationships, career, health—that is often when we're motivated to step up, harness our voices, and demand to be heard. We need to get to this point of

59 "National Health Expenditure Data," Centers for Medicare and Medicaid Services, last modified December 11, 2018, https://www.cms.gov/research-statistics-data-and-systems/statistics-trends-and-reports/nationalhealthexpenddata/nationalhealthaccountshistorical.html.

desperation with our healthcare, and I think we're at that point, to motivate us and propel us into action. Sometimes we need to get just sick enough to force ourselves out of our comfort zones and venture into the unknown. This is the Healthcare Hero's Journey: it's off the beaten path, it's scary, and there are risks. The rewards, however, can drastically benefit all areas of our lives long term.

As this book was readying for print, things did, in fact, get bad. When the COVID-19 pandemic began sweeping the globe, the US healthcare system was quickly strained beyond its limits. Overwhelmed by demand, care centers, labs, and providers struggled to keep up or effectively quarantine. Combined with limited testing options, barriers and delays mounted and led to potentially infected patients not getting the care they needed. Within weeks, Americans were in crisis, as was the healthcare system.

Responding to the urgent need for better access to coronavirus screening, myLAB Box launched our COVID-19 at-home test for clinics, doctor offices, and pharmacies nationwide, followed by a direct-to-consumer test. Our test offered the invaluable opportunity to diagnose, treat, and quarantine simultaneously and meant a lower risk of spreading the infection among the public and healthcare professionals.

By opening sales to professional healthcare providers first, we aimed to alleviate some of the challenges they struggled with, which allowed them to better serve their patients anytime and anywhere, even in self-quarantine. Despite its burden on our healthcare system and economy, it is my hope that this crisis will propel us to take action.

Doing something as small as caring for myself and advocating for my health spurred my professional life and ultimately led me to found the first of its kind healthcare start-up: myLAB Box. When myLAB Box started, we faced a lot of skepticism, but we persevered and proved the skeptics wrong. Now there are other companies in the space who use a similar formula to deliver their own goods and services. Rather than feel threatened, I'm excited. As long as the vision is being accomplished, it doesn't have to be myLAB Box accomplishing it. The way we change how healthcare processes work is to have multiple companies doing it at the same time. As a business owner, I'm always asking myself how I can differentiate my company and how I can make it bigger and better. What's next? As we decide what our business evolutions will be, our efforts will continue to center around empowering people to live better and more joyous lives while connecting with the world, community, and themselves in healthier ways.

Learning how to advocate for my own healthcare and my own well-being created a ripple effect throughout so many areas of my life. Even in my relationships, I gauge a potential partner's desire to be active and healthy. I've noticed that I am happier when I am more selective because I've had relationships with people who were the opposite of me. I found myself hiking and biking alone. It was changing who I was. Since I've become more aware about my own imperatives to change, I've learned that it's actually always been important for me to have a partner who will participate with me in healthy activities.

I've also noticed that once I made my health and well-being a priority, my friends did as well. I used to see friends for dinner or drinks. Now they call me when they want to go hiking or for a walk on the beach. This wasn't even an intended outcome. As I talked more excitedly about the activities I was engaging in, some of them started asking to join. This is evidence that any kind of behavior makes the people around us more likely to choose the same behavior. This shows us that when it comes to health advocacy, we don't have to find new friends and support systems; we just have to be patient with and supportive of our current ones.

Authors of *Connected* researched this phenomenon and found that "mathematical analysis of the network suggests that a person is about 15 percent more likely to be happy if a directly connected person (at one degree of separation) is happy."[60] As surprising as this causal effect seems to be, authors Christakis and Fowler tie it back to our own biology: "Emotions spread from person to person because of two features of human interaction: we are biologically hardwired to mimic others outwardly, and in mimicking their outward displays, we come to adopt their inward states."[59] The valuable takeaway from this research and my own experience is that how you feel and act impacts the people around you, whether they are your friends, partners, children, coworkers. Understand that your mood, and your health choices, will affect the health and choices of everybody else around you. If you won't do it for you, do it for them. Sometimes we care about other people more than we care about ourselves. Some of us were told at an early age that taking care of ourselves is selfish. Rather than thinking of self-care as taking time away from others, think of it as investing time in teaching them how to care for themselves lovingly.

On a macroscale, we should be concerned by and engaged with what is happening to our healthcare system. On a microscale, we should be focused on loving our children, partners, families, friends, and last but never least, ourselves. What we know is that all of these are interconnected. We are unified by our singularity. Your body cannot be healthy if one organ malfunctions. As reported in *Connected*, "A key factor in determining our health is the health of others."[59] Apply that principle on a larger scale: Is your family healthy if you are sick? Is your city healthy if you are sick? Is your community healthy if you

---

60 Nicholas Christakis and James Fowler, *Connected: The Surprising Power of Our Social Networks and How They Shape Our Lives* (New York: Little, Brown and Company, 2009), 51, 37, 130.

are sick? Is your country healthy if you are sick? Is your world healthy if you are sick?

Speaking up for ourselves is a trait that tends to empower us in more ways than one. People who speak up for themselves at the doctor's office are more likely to advocate for themselves at work and at home. When you develop self-advocacy skills in any of these areas, it automatically impacts all of your interactions. Even though we are focusing on health advocacy, this comes down to self-appreciation, self-respect, and self-awareness. Imagine what integrating these traits can do for our society, our healthcare space, our culture.

There is a new trend toward advocacy building in our culture driven by a new generation. They are not different by nature, but their access to media and their ability to use their influence as a tool has given them the unique ability to mobilize in numbers like we've never seen before. This trend shows that if we set a positive example, it has a trickle-down effect. It also shows the power of taking action, no matter your age. Regardless of your demographics, you have the power, capacity, and ability to advocate for yourself effectively. You can't let anything hold you back. Advocacy is saying *no* to anyone who says you are not old enough, smart enough, powerful enough to deserve the best.

We've pointed out the problems with our current system, and the solution is simple: we need to take action. Take action with your health choices, your votes cast, your purchases made, your standards set. If you are reading this book, you are likely already thinking about taking action or at least thinking about asking for help. Both of these actions show strength and are extremely important in changing outcomes.

The revolution of the healthcare industry starts with you. My hope is that you will use the advocacy skills discussed in this book to be your own advocate in all realms of your life—health, career, and relational. Advocacy is a muscle, and it needs training. Speaking up is a trait that empowers us in more ways than one. If we can become a generation of informed and outspoken patients, we have the power to change the system. Using the tools and techniques in the book, create your own Dr. You, who can be a tireless advocate for your health and well-being. Health is certainly a goal of this book, but empowerment is an even greater takeaway. May your confidence in yourself—in Dr. You—extend into all realms of your life, so that you can be healthy and whole to live the life you want.

THE REVOLUTION OF THE HEALTHCARE INDUSTRY STARTS WITH YOU.